WHO'S IN CHARGE???

WHO'S IN CHARGE???

Peggy Lee

AuthorHouse™
1663 Liberty Drive
Bloomington, IN 47403
www.authorhouse.com
Phone: 1-800-839-8640

Published by AuthorHouse 12/27/2012

ISBN: 978-1-4772-9929-6 (sc)
ISBN: 978-1-4772-9928-9 (e)

Library of Congress Control Number: 2012923646

This book is printed on acid-free paper.

Thanks to Peggy S. Lee, my mom. I recently just became unfocused. I thought at times you didn't pay me any attention. At that moment that I needed words of encouragement, out of no where, you reminded me that I suppose to be writing and not to give up. Thank you Quecyon, Saquiss and Timothy, for being the loves of my life. You make me want to do my best. I want to give you my all. I hope I encourage you in some way, to want to accomplish your goals and dreams. Mommy loves you.

To all the little people that I've met. It was good meeting you and I pray the best for you all. I had fun with you.

BONUS JOURNAL ENTRY

THE HYPOCHONDRIAC MASOCHIST

For the first time in over ten years, I had a couple of slots available, just looking to fill just one. But, if I could fill both slots, awesome.

I inquired other centers and providers if they could refer me to potential clients, that they have no room for.

Of course, no one will be quick to help a stranger. The owner of Daddy Day Care did. We talked. We laughed. We communicated.

From the outside, her house looked huge. Her yard definitely was. It was fenced in, with play gyms, swing set and other outdoor activity equipment.

Her house set on the main street, with a large sign that displayed her daycare name, hours, ages accepted and number. I figured she would always get some form of business. She's on the main street.

I was right.

She called me one day and informed me that she had someone whom just left her house looking for daycare service. She referred the family to me. They were on their way to my house.

I thanked her. A few months later, I called her and asked what the hell did she send to my house. Joking on how I delivered the question, but, seriously wanting to know the answer.

She came with her daughter and friend.

"Hi." I greeted them at the door. We shook hands.

"Hi. How are you?" She responded.

"Wait, wait. What's wrong?" I frantically asked.

Her three year old daughter ran straight through the house. She ran right passed us all and literally jumped on the stove. Yes, she did. She jumped, then continued to pull herself up from the handle of the oven door.

"You can't do that, sweetie?"

"I'm sorry. That's why I need to get her in daycare. The daycare she was at, just didn't do anything with them. They were allowed to do whatever they wanted. Except for her, it was all boys there. She's a tomboy."

"Oh, okay. Well, she can be a tomboy, but, she can't go around behaving like that."

"Do you think you can handle her? She's a hand full."

"She's not a problem. We're structured here. I can get her out of that. We do work here. They have play time, and free timc but, they have to sit at a table and in chairs and do their activity for the day."

The two friends were in awe over the layout of my daycare room. It was set up just like a preschool setting.

"Do you have room for one more? Because, I have a son."

"Yes. But, I would have to meet him. I have room for him.

My interview process is that the parents bring their children with them so that we all could meet, before their first day.

I wouldn't want them to be too uncomfortable, being dropped off at a stranger's house for the first time without meeting me first."

"Oh he's quiet. He's a mini me. He's shy and don't bother no one. They always picked with him at the other daycare and would hit on him all of the time."

"He'll be fine here. I have a son around his age. They sound alike. Only no one picks with him or bothers him. He's a nice boy. He laughs with his little friends. So, he'll be okay."

Within the first couple of weeks, her son punched my son in the nose, for not wanting to play with him.

She started coming to me of tales of chasing down another daycare provider. Just out of the blue moon. Telling me weird stories. I wasn't nor would I ever do anything wrong to anyone's child. So, I couldn't figure out if she was subliminally sending me a message.

She started acting crazier than a lab monkey. I would hear the door close behind her, after she picked up her kids and left.

"Mommy, their car is still in front of our house."

"Oh, maybe she's doing something." I said although it's been 10 minutes since she left.

"I don't see their mom."

"What! Let me go see what's going on out there."

I walked toward the steps to the daycare door. She was standing up against the wall holding onto the sign-in clipboard, rocking.

I would quickly step back to see what the freak she was doing. She wouldn't say anything. She'll just leave, without even signing out.

I heard screaming outside of my house one day after they left.

"Mommy! Mommy! something happened in front of the house. I think the daycare kids got hit by a car!"

"All the daycare kids are gone!"

I looked out of the front window. Oh my greatness! It's my daycare kid's mom, screaming at the top of her lungs. She's running around her car, that's in the middle of the street. I don't see anyone from my view. I grabbed a bat. I ran out of the other door.

"What's wrong?!" I'm frantically looking around. Who's after her, I'm questioning in my head.

"Help! Help me!"

"What!" I'm looking into the car. I see the two daycare kids—her kids. They appear to be fine. The little girl is standing up in the car, watching her mother run. Her brother is sitting on the edge of the sit, doing the same.

"I don't know how to help you. Tell me what's wrong. I don't see no one."

"Oh my God! It's a bee in the car!"

That went on for ten or fifteen minutes. I went in the house, after laughing from shock. Once we all did, neighbors also, she got in the car and drove off like nothing happened.

It's after eleven in the evening. It's almost time for the two kids to leave. I hear tapping at the door. Then, I heard shaking of the doorknob. I am about to call the police.

Now, there's knocking at the door.

"Why didn't you open the door for me?" she asked while standing outside of the door. "I could have gotten killed."

"Huh?"

Suddenly, she started screaming for her life. She ran up into the house knocking me up against the wall. I yanked her out of the way so that I could close and lock my doors. I was scared.

"What, somebody out there? Somebody following you? What's wrong?" I asked peeking through the curtains.

"It's a dog across the street."

This went on for a little over a year. Then it was bye-bye for her ass. I acted like I couldn't accommodate her any longer. I said I had no way to get to the bus stop, although it was just a street away.

She on the other hand was questioning bringing her kids back, because it was time for the little girl to start school soon. She said she didn't want her to hurt herself walking. No, no the little girl didn't have any handicaps.

Before they left, she had us paranoid. She had my family peeking out of the windows.

I had to have people come over at times when it was time for her to pick up. She was over the top.

She would get a scratch somewhere on her body, the next day she would think she had a disease and swore that Jesus Christ came and told her she was dying.

Before her daughter calmed down and became a little lady, she supposedly hurt herself, at my house.

She was trying to jump down the basement stairs. I grabbed her by her left arm. I told her mom of her misbehaving. The next day and week went like this.

"What time do you get off, Miss. Peggy?"

"I don't know. Why?"

"I can't go to work. I have to take my daughter to the emergency."

I gasped. The emergency room. That's scrious. The mom had a whine in her voice.

"What's wrong? Is she ok? She just left here two hours ago. She was fine."

"Yeah. I took her to a Neo Clinic. They said she had a hairline fracture in her wrist. But, I don't think they took enough x-rays. So, I'm taking her to the E.R."

"What happened to her wrist?"

"They said it happened when you grabbed her."

“What! I don’t think so. I didn’t grab her by her wrist.”

She didn’t take her to the doctor. She drop them off and told me that her daughter said, that, her arm was really hurting her. For the sake of her crazy minded mama, I wrapped her arm in an ace bandage.

The next day she was back at it.

“Are you going to come up to the Children’s Hospital?” she called me on the phone and asked.

“What is wrong with you? Why would I come to the hospital?”

“It’s your fault that I have to bring my daughter up here. The doctor said you made her injury worse by wrapping the bandage on her.”

“I don’t think so, sweetheart—impossible.”

“Yes he did!” she responded hastily.

The next day she came with her arm in a snoopy sling.

“What happened to the baby arm?” I asked while taking a picture. I’m not stupid. That girl was psychotic.

“They said when you pulled her by her arm when she was falling down the stairs over here, you pulled her elbow out of socket. I’m glad I went to that hospital. My baby gotta be in that sling for six weeks.”

“Well, I know they didn’t tell you that. I grabbed her by her upper arm. Her back was up against the wall and the only arm available for me to grab was her left arm. Her right arm is in a sling."

The mother yelled at her daughter, telling her she better not try to jump down the stairs again.

Two days later the little girl was doing cartwheels—without the sling.

"You know she still supposed to have it on, but, it was the Fourth of July weekend and it didn't go with her outfit. So, I just didn't put it back on her. Her arm was probably hurting from when her cousin picked her up and swung her across the room when she was a baby.

It was time for school to start. I asked her for the little boy's bus schedule.

"They didn't give me a schedule. They said it could come anywhere from 2pm through 3:30pm."

"No. Everyone has to have a schedule. I'm not going by no hours like that. You're going to have to make sure."

She couldn't confirm it. I went to pick the little boy up, from his bus stop two days later. The other parents standing out there with me confirmed it. Those hours of bus drop off time is opened like that. But, they're usually dropped off by 2:45pm.

The next week. The kids weren't supposed to be at my house until 4:30pm. I hear the phone ringing.

"Hello."

"Miss. Peggy what time the bus come?"

"I don't know. I usually get him before 3pm. But, like you all said it comes when it wants to."

"Oh, I'ma pick him up. I just want to know when to be there."

I didn't know why she was telling me. I wasn't picking him up. They weren't supposed to be in my care at that time.

A little while later the phone began to ring off the hook.

I'm not answering it. I didn't have anyone at my facility. My morning family left at noon.

Now, I hear frantic horn honking outside. My phone is ringing.

I go outside.

"Hey. Look at you looking nice. I like those capris you have on."

"Thanks."

"Where you get them from?"

"At a some store out in Akron?"

"What you doing here this early?"

Suddenly, she went mad.

"I can't find my son!"

"What! What do you mean?"

"You told me to pick him up at 3 o'clock!"

"I didn't tell you that. I said I usually get him from his bus stop by three."

"You made me loose my son!"

"Girl. Go back to the bus stop. You said you never told him where your new house was. But, he's ten years old. He knows where you live. He showed me. Maybe he walked home. It's only a couple of blocks over."

"He's not. You going to have to come help me look for him. It's your fault, that I went looking around in the stores. I thought I had time to look around and do some shopping. You told me 3 o'clock."

All along after the kids were dropped off at 4:30 that late afternoon, she had picked him up already. She saw him walking down the street, according to the little boy and dropped him off at home. Yet, felt the need to act a damn nut at my house.

You see I showed him how to walk to his house. She showed him and told him to walk to my house, in the case that no one was there to pick him up. That's what he did on several occasions, even when he wasn't supposed to be at my house at all, that day. Even if hc was supposed to come later that day, he wasn't coming before hand. I wouldn't allow it. At times I would be off and he'd show up.

The next week she felt the need to be ignorant. I went to pick her child up from the bus stop. He wasn't there. I waited until 3pm. The bus never came no later than that.

I went back to the house. I had another family dropping off. I called his school. I introduced myself. I was looking for my daycare child, who's not at the bus stop.

They informed me that they couldn't give me any information. I wasn't down as a contact person and I wasn't the parent or guardian. But, the buses had all came back. The bus driver dropped off the last set of kids at 2:40pm.

I called the mother. She wouldn't answer. I left by foot with all the other kids, to go back to the bus stop.

While waiting at the light, a car drives slowly pass us. I noticed the little boy. I yelled out his name. I yelled for the car to stop.

"Hey that's my daycare child! Why you have him in your car?!"

I asked while opening up the car door.

"This my nephew."

I asked the ten year to confirm it. He said she was his auntie.

"I'm sorry if I scared you. My sister told me to pick him up for some reason."

"What?!"

"She said she wasn't sure if you were going to pick him up. I told her to call you and let you know that I was picking him up. She didn't tell you?"

"No."

PHASE ONE

HERE WE GO AGAIN

Somewhere in the book; Who's Keeping Your Children? Wouldn't You Like To Know?—I wrote about past experiences working with families and their children.

I also wrote of some changes that needed to occur in my business and personal aspects of my life. As I tap my pen on this note pad reflecting back to the beginning of my changes, I realize haven't a damn thing changed. Except for a few things; the children, the parents and the days. The experience, well, hey, the experiences are like life, iffy, but explosive at times.

I don't know what's going on. I need to be evaluated sometimes I think to myself. I don't play baseball. Nevertheless, it seems as though someone put me in center field, without a damn bat or mitt—just throwing balls at me every which a way. That's what I have to deal with everyday—not protected or sheltered by nothing, but people approaching me with balls.

Now what am I supposed to do? What are you going to do? When someone come to your place of business, acting as if they're head in charge, in your establishment.

No disrespect to myself. Like, I know you're not trying to disrespect yourself, by agreeing that if anyone is going to be bold and out of line if need to be, it's going to be you—THE REAL F****** ONE IN CHARGE.

Oh, I'm sorry. Excuse me I hope you didn't think that this was going to be some sugar and spice and all girls are nice type of book. You got the wrong skirt. Remember what I said in the first book.

Everything in the world, including the world itself, has some form of lining to keep it together—to hold it together, to keep its' functions running strong. When that lining begins thinning, that thing starts to lose its' durability, its' worthiness. You start doubting its' capabilities. So, you decide to put up the detour sign, the temporarily out of service sign, the under construction sign; while it still has a chance to be repaired, fixed up, strengthened up, remodeled to its' best abilities. Before it thins so much it breaks and cause un-repairable damages.

I'm one of those things in the world, a human being, that has a lining. Although I'm not touching that thin line yet, I'm just steps away. That's to close for me. So, I think that it's time for me to put up my detour sign, my temporarily out of service sign, my under construction sign, my out to lunch sign, before I even begin to see signs of thinning. See, the line that I need to reconstruct, before it even begins to thin just a little bit, is the line that keeps me sane.

If I allow my line of sanity to thin, even if it's just a little bit, so will every line in me that gives me strength and keeps me going, will also thin. If I lose a pinch of sanity, I jeopardize my entire livelihood. My position as a mother, parent, sister, an auntie, daughter, a friend, a person of patience and tolerance, a rational person, me as a woman, me as a childcare provider will be in question.

My sanity must be strong at all times in order for my mental, emotional, physical and social capabilities can be trusted. By me first, then by the people that surrounds me. A lot of us fail to realize these capabilities of ours is a packaged deal. If one breaks down, so will the other ones. How can one do anything or be trusted in that state?

It would take me several years to realize that no one cares about your state of mind. They definitely don't care if you, yourself don't show signs of caring about yourself or caring about your time, or about your family.

I've always said to myself, I'm going to help out with these families. I'm going to be the best provider, they've ever met. I'm going to make sure they know that I'm here for them. If they need to work some extra hours, that's fine with me; as long as they're trying to do something positive for themselves and their families.

I'd also come to realize, that these people are out for nothing but themselves. It sometimes seems to me that these people don't even care if their children gets wholesome care, as long as they don't have to be bothered with their kids. No matter what I do or how much I do for these people and their families, It'll never be enough. They'll never be satisfied. No matter how many times I bend over backwards for these people and their children, my services would never be appreciated.

I'd realize over and over again, that I've been a fool and I'll be a damn fool, if I continue to be a childcare provider and not take a long over due break; after having reminiscence of some anxiety attacking times.

So Here I Go With My Therapy.

A lot of people are fooled by one's appearance; be it the physical formation, or the mental manipulation of good conversation, or the blindness of one's pure desperation. Outside of me not wanting anyone to look after my children, I didn't want to have to pay someone to abuse my children. That was my frame of thinking. Being blind from being desperate, is the position that I felt that I would be in. Those thoughts out of many, would be why I'd become a home childcare provider.

I would have never imagine what a calamity it would truly be, having strangers invade my life with their lifestyles; their downfalls, relationships, their sickness, the abuse and neglect in their lives, their smiles and their tears and so much more. The business will become the invasion in my home (which will soon just be a house), in my life as well as my children's. My social life began to deteriorate, right before me, what little it was that existed, without my knowledge, without me even knowing it was taking place.

Did that happen to you yet? Did it? I mean, to where you're so involved in these people that's come into your home, that you forget you exist. Your children are longing for your attention, so is your mate. Family and friends begins to exclude you from functions, since you always seem to be wrapped up in your daycare business. So wrapped up in fact, you fail to recognize the deceit that's occurring around you. To busy trying to get that stamp of approval.

Many people feel as though this is a sit down job. They say it's simple, anyone could do it. I've heard people say that's not even a job; you don't do shit—put them to bed for half the day is all you would have to do. They're so crazy and so wrong. I'll make my mental remarks to myself, when I hear people make goofy remarks about home childcare providers. It'll be several years later, when I'd make my remarks out loud; to anyone who seems to have unappreciated comments.

Umm, tis-tis-tis. I don't know who set in motion, the let's test the provider, to see how much she really can take, game. I personally don't like taking test. I could know every answer to each question, thus, still lose my cools. Like, I know I will and you would too, soon, if you had to go through this.

PHASE TWO

RISE AND SHINE

The sound of the alarm clock was buzzing through my ears. The red alarm clock read 6:20am. I had forty minutes to myself before I had to wake up my three children, to get them ready for school. I had and hour and forty minutes to myself before a childcare child was dropped off at my house.

I sat up on my queen sized bed, my hands cupping my face. I looked over at my closet. The doors were already opened. I glanced at all the clothes that were hanging up and folded on the shelves, nothing fancy, though.

I walked over and touched a few different fabrics of clothing, knowing damn well I wouldn't be wearing either one, I touched or viewed. I reached down in the laundry basket that set in the corner of my room and picked out a nice outfit for the occasion—keeping someone else's children.

I picked out a pajama shirt that was now just a long pink shirt, the picture of the . . . wait, I don't know what the picture was of. I just know it faded off a long time ago. I bought several of these long t-shirts with prints, that came down to your knees practically, from Medic Drug Store. I reached for a pair of suede jogging pants, when I went into deep thought. This is ridiculous. These suede pants was supposed to be something to compliment my silhouette of divineness, now just covers up my oops.

Suede, my first suede anything, well it felt like suede, when I first bought it. It didn't feel the same. I washed and wore them so much it felt and looked like the original state of material before they were pants, cotton with the pricks.

It wasn't a problem since I felt like a slave anyway. "Yessa, Isa bees ready soon massa to clean yos kids nasty little nose and change their filthy little diapers and wait for you to treats me like I'ma dumb ass.

After getting ready I sipped a little coffee and got ready to walk my kids to their bus stop. It was now 8:20am. No one had showed up yet, not even called to say they were running late. They know I leave out at eight thirty. Just then, one client showed up.

"Good Morning." I greeted but didn't get a response, although I'm right in this parent's face.

Sometimes I repeat myself, if I'm upstairs from the side door that they enter. I know that they hear me. They're just being ignorant at times. Sometimes I can be ignorant and not speak at all until they speak. After all, they're entering my damn house they're supposed to speak when they're entering anyway. I am the professional one. I thought when you enter anyone's house you're to speak.

"Y'all about to leave?"

"Yes, we are."

"Where y'all going? Because she has on heels and I don't want her messing up her shoes or falling down scratching up her legs."

"Oh, well I have to walk my kids to their bus stop."

"What, they're to big for you to still be taking them to school. My daughter don't want to go anyway."

I laughed it off.

"You're funny. But, I have to go before they're late."

"Well I need you to change her shoes."

"What?"

"I left her some play shoes over here. She gotta put those on her before she leaves."

"Oh, no, I don't have time for that. It's eight thirty-one."

I wanted to tell her, you change her shoes yourself. Didn't no one tell you to put no two inch wedge heels on a three year old, anyway.

It's always someone or that one thing that sets off the domino effect. It seems like it.

"Go get that other bag of candy out of my room. And, you better close my door." I instructed one of my own kids to do.

Usually, they'd argue about who's going to do what. I'd have to mediate.

This time around, I knew they'd all try to get to that bag of Easter candy—to sneak a piece.

I was already on the porch. All of my morning children were here, except for one. I assumed she wasn't coming considering it was in the nine o'clock hour. One of my rules was: no service if over an hour late. Even with a phone call you have within your scheduled hour to drop off.

Although it was a nice day in April, the Friday before Easter Sunday, it became a little breezy, nothing to go in the house over. I was about to, but one my kids asked if I wanted a sweater. I said yes. So, my son bought it out to me, along with a pair of socks. I was bare footed.

We should have went in the got-damn house. I looked up and notice the family that was late and shouldn't have even come, arriving that late, over four hours.

In my heart of hearts I still wanted to go inside the house—wait for them to knock and not answer. Or tell them it was too late for drop off. I get sick and tired of these people doing what the F* * * they want to do.

But—but . . . although I was trying to act as if I didn't see them pull up by continuing to stuff the plastic eggs with different candies, I couldn't help but notice the semi-naked child in front of me.

I looked up through my glasses, thinking to myself *why didn't they fix up her clothes. She must have on a dress that rose above her waist.*

Then, I lift my head up to see clearly, 'cause I know damn well I don't see what I see.

"Gook Morning." I greeted the cashew complexioned woman, that was trying to keep a grip on the little girl whom was wiggling in her arms.

"I'm running late, girl."

"I noticed."

"Get that bag out the car now! She gripped at the little girls' brother.

"Where's her shoes and socks?"

"Everything is in the bag. Give her that bag. That's for you."

As she was walking up the steps with the little girl to put her down, her grandson was handing me the gift bag.

"What does this supposed to be?" I asked with a raised brow.

"Her mother told me to give you that for the baby. So she can't stay out here. It's getting kind of windy."

"You better put your sister's clothes on." I said to the ten year old.

"You told me I can't change her."

"I said you can't change her pamper while you're over here. But you better put her clothes on inside that doorway, because I'm not about to go in no house to get anyone ready."

"Hurry up and put her clothes on!" she huffed at her grandson.

The grandmother came from the side door where she had to sign in. I know she heard me. I wanted her to hear me.

Who brings a one year old (I don't care how old) to daycare with a little t-shirt and rain coat on and that's it. Giving the provider a gift bag—me a gift bag, having me think I'm getting an appreciation gift, for my hard work. **Yes-the-hell-I-did-deserve a gift.** Do you know what I do, neglect, over look, disregard, what I give, over extend? Instead, I'm approached with a beautiful bag with a new outfit in it, for the one year old.

We've all gone beyond our duties before—many times in this line of profession. You have to stand back to see what you're really doing, to gain knowledge and wisdom of growth and enabling.

Now I know of this provider who dresses her daycare children. She even went as far as going to buy products for their hair. I mean she went too damn far. If she wasn't going to purchase grease and shampoo to wash, grease and braid a child's hair—she was parting and putting a special shampoo in the child's scalp for the treatment of lice.

Grant it, that, it was different occasions, but, each occasion to me was beyond ones' duty. Especially, when you're doing things like this and your business comes from most of the time word of mouth. Some people will come, not for your credentials in childcare, yet, for the responsibility you're willing to take off of their hands. That will blow up in your face. I should know.

You want to know why I'm writing this runner-up to the first book; "Who's Keeping Your Children?" "Wouldn't You Like To Know?" Something drastically had happened since then. Our children access to education has been stolen. Schools all around is closing their doors. School buildings are being knocked down unknown to school authorities when they'll rebuild.

Teachers are being laid off by the dozen. Teachers are walking away from their positions. Transportation to take our children to the school—a school that for now is still opened, is limited or not available at all.

School hours in some areas vary by the year. On top of all the school issues people have to worry about keeping their job positions.

All this is leaving parents more desperate now more than ever. It seems like people have a lot on their plates lately, that makes it damn near impossible to juggle through all of those strenuous hurdles of life.

This in my opinion is going to become a big issue for providers, centers and nannies. Either some are not going to care who's keeping their children or they're damn near going to make sure you feel as though you damn near agreed to adopt their children.

It's sad—so sad. But, you now what, I-don't-give-a-damn!

We are all going through the same damn thing—some issues less of a concern than most. You're not that stressful. If you have time to do things for yourself, like going drinking some where, clubbing and getting your ass or balls wet—that you have to put your responsibilities off on someone else.

My phone was ringing off the hook. I couldn't answer it right then and there. I had pampers to change. That right there takes a while, if you have more than one child in a pamper. You have to clean the child, change the pamper, put their clothes back on, disinfect the area, wash your hands and start the procedure all over again.

"Hello. Good Morning."

"Hey Ms. Lady. What's going on?"

"Um . . . nothing." I dragged out of my mouth.

"This is Martha."

"Oh, hey. You sound different."

"I'm mad as hell, that's why."

"Aw, what's wrong?"

"Remember I told you that I had this new family—where the mother said that she's going to have to find someone else or a new job, because she's always late to work.

"Yeah."

"Now, remember I told you that I told her I'd pick her kids up myself from her house at 6:30 in the morning, instead of her dropping off at my house at seven. Because, I have to be up and ready to get my own kids to school by 7:30 in the morning.

"Uh, huh, don't she live up the street from you?"

"Girl yeah."

"Now, how was she always late?"

"Wait a minute, I'm about to get to all of that. She told me that she had to catch the bus to work, since her car was down. So hell, I don't want her to be late. What's thirty extra minutes. I'll pick up the kids myself."

"So, why are you pissed off, again?"

"Not only does this flakey faced fool not catch the bus, she's driving around in a truck, a nice one. And, not only doesn't this ugly thang goes to work late she doesn't have to be to work until 10 o'clock. That scalawag told me she had to work from eight until four. So, I was keeping them from seven to five, well 6:30am to 5pm."

"Didn't you read her placement letter? Doesn't it tell you her hours?"

"She told me she had to get another one, because the other provider from the last month wouldn't give it to her."

"How did you find out, anyway?"

"Huh, how did I find out? After I dropped my kids off at school, I went to get me and her kids something to eat. Guess who I saw sitting in McDonalds looking all chipper, across the table from her little boyfriend?"

"Ha, ha, ha, their mother."

"That shit ain't funny. I drove right out of that drive-thru . . . went home . . . fixed them some oatmeal and got the number to her worker.

When I called downtown and gave them the workers ID number from the voucher, that's how I found out about her hours.

The worker just so happened to answer the doggon phone, cause you know those people don't be answering those phones. They just let them ring. Her worker was real nice. I told her that this girl said she could never get in touch with her, in order to get an updated placement letter with my name on it.

I told her about my arrangement too and how I saw her. She went on about me not losing my license and went ahead and looked up her information."

"Puh-leeze, I would have took them in there and got me that 2 for $3 Mcgriddle deal—set at the table next to her and said, "Good Morning, your kids didn't eat."

"No, I'm just not going to get them at no six thirty. Oh, did I tell you her worker said that she worked part-time from 10am-2pm? I've been keeping them from 6:30a.m. to five in the evening. Mind you, each time that I picked them up, she gave me their clothes in a bag, talking about she wouldn't have time to change them.

See what I'm sayin."

"No, but I hear you."

You could pretty much tell what type of characteristics a person have just by being their childcare provider. If you need to know what type of woman or a man is, ask the childcare provider. If you want to know if a certain person would be a good mother to your child/ children, ask the provider.

I kid you not. I can't believe what I see with my own eyes. To hear with my own ears of stories from providers of their experiences with different families. It's—it's a fable. These things are made up.

For dozens, if not hundreds of providers at some point in time in our line of business, it is and will be—unbelievable experiences.

It's amazing when you're congregating amongst each other and telling the same stories. You would have thought that all of these providers were reading from the same script or happen to be keeping the same families.

It seems and I said it seems as though no one wants to do anything with or for their children.

Provider:	Hi, you don't have to take her coat off.
Parent:	Okay. You going somewhere?
Provider:	You know I have to drop my other daycare children off at school.
Parent:	Bye mommies baby. She said as she pulled her daughter off of her hips and put her on the floor.
Provider:	Um, wait a minute, where's her clothes?
Parent:	Oh, it's in her bag.
Provider:	No. No you're going to have to take her home and change her.
Parent:	I don't have time to do all of that.
Provider:	I have to leave, sweetheart. I can't get these children to school late, just so I can dress someone else's child.
Parent:	Well, she has on a footed sleeper. And, besides you gone be in the car anyway.
Provider:	It doesn't matter if her sleeper covers her feet or whether we're in a car. This is inappropriate. Would you take her to a center dress like this?
Parent:	That's different.

You wouldn't believe how many times I had to tell someone to bring their children to daycare dressed. There hasn't been a year yet, that I haven't had someone come to my facility expecting me to wash and dress their child.

Or, I have to tell someone to dress their children appropriate. No matter what, no matter what you say, someone always seem to show up acting as if it's the providers responsibility to dress their child.

Provider: Hello, this is she. My daughter did what? Okay I'll be there. I'll be there in thirty minutes. I have to wait for my afternoon daycare families to arrive and I'll be right there.

She made arrangements to meet with her daughter's teacher. Moments later, one of the families arrived.

Parent: Hi, I'm going to sign in and I'll see you tonight. Oh yeah, her sock and shoes are in her bag.

Provider: Okay, then you're going to have to put them on her.

Parent: She's not going to let me put them on without having a fit. I'll be late trying to do all of that.

Provider: You better hurry up.

Parent: She'll be okay without them. She's only fourteen months. It's not like she's going to be walking around.

Provider: Does she know how to walk?

Parent: Yeah, but . . . you can't put them on for me? She snickered.

Provider: I just got three kids things on. You're just getting here.

There's no reason why I should be getting her dressed.

You'd hear a lot of providers say that in order for them to keep their business afloat they have to kiss ass. In some manner I believe that.

Just like I believe, that, if a personn realize that they could pretty much say or suggest something abnormal, out of the way, that they wouldn't normally address neither to a center or to school staff members, towards their mama, they'll do it in a heartbeat. You're wrapped around their little finger—they know it, too. You'd go for it—would you?

Unfortunately, we're in some kind of spoof. No one knows why or how we're here. Each year there's something new to experience.

I'm under the assumption that the way we run our business is the way we run our lives. I'd be the first to admit, at times I'm as firm as a concreted sidewalk. Which we all know, will eventually crack.

Provider: Why is he still in his sleeper?

Parent: Oh, I put his clothes in the diaper bag.

Provider: Didn't I tell you guys, that, all kids supposed to be dressed and presentable, before they're dropped off?

Parent: I don't have time to do all of that, in the morning. You work from home. I didn't see it as being a big deal, for you to dress him.

Provider: Really, did you really think I was going to dress your son? You need to read the regulations that's posted on the door. She informed in a soft manner tone.

The parent read a portion of the rules that were posted. She huffed and puffed, as she shoved the ten month old in the arms of the provider, who was standing by the door she was propping open with her foot. The parent stormed down the walkway, stopped and turn to address the provider.

Parent: I'm just going to find someone else to keep my son, if you can't help me out. You expecting me to do things that I shouldn't even have to do. That's what you fo, know what I'm sayin' How you gone say you ain't gone open up the door if my child aint' dress the way you want him to be dress. That's some . . . man.

Provider: First of all, if you feel that you need to replace a good childcare provider because I'm not willing to dress your child for you . . . his mother, then by all means put in your notice today. Secondly, no child is to come to my facility undressed for the day in pajamas, yesterday clothes, overnight nothing.

Lastly, I keep your child so that you could go to school or to work. I . . . knock on wood, try to keep your son out of harms way. I feed your child more meals than you feed him. I do activities with your child. I know my position, know yours.

Don't forget to pick up on time and have a nice day.

Her irritation was exposed.

You really have to pay attention to these parents coming into your home, your place of business. A lot of providers just open and close their doors. They do the where is childcare schedule; where's the kids, the vouchers and or money. They don't do any kind of communication with people dropping off.

You have to know when to cut them off and when to let them continue to talk. That goes for the individuals they have picking up the kids. They would know something that the parent wouldn't tell or want you to know.

You all better listen. You'll find out where your money is. Why isn't it being paid in full or on time, or if you need to replace them (the family) and if they're trying to replace you for whatever reason.

STORY TIME

WHAT TIME IS IT?

"I can't wait until tomorrow." I said to a few of my associates. We were planning to get together, late the next day, on Friday.

"What time you want me to come pick you up?"

"My last parent picks up at eleven, eleven-twenty at the latest. So . . . what . . . eleven-thirty, eleven forty-five."

"Are you sure? Don't have me drive all the way over there for nothing."

"Yeah. Why would I have you come out that time of night for nothing? Better yet, to my house—Lamont."

"Who is Lamont?" "The son from the Sanford and Son show, you big dummy." We laughed over the phone. Then disconnected to touch basics with the others that were also getting off somewhat late on Friday—who hadn't been out for a while and was also, excited about getting out. One also was a provider, one a former provider and the other was a nurse—her friend was a cook.

The day seemed to drag on. It was Friday, but not Friday. For some reason Friday only meant something at six o'clock in the evening. All of my daycare kids were gone by five, except for the two little girls that came at twelve noon and the other at five thirty, my second shift.

Quite time was at seven o'clock, which means no running around, no loud talking, no activities that consist of too much energy. They could read, put together puzzles, watch t.v. Whatever, long as it wasn't loud. Eight o'clock was rest time, lay down, be quite, don't talk to me unless it's an emergency.

From this time until their parents picked them up, belonged to me, my kids, cleaning, my meal time, freshening up, talking on the phone—whatever I wanted to do.

On this particular evening I wanted to go out, something I rarely get a chance to do and that's hang out with adults. I'm excited . . . until . . .

"I'd let that bitch go." the person on the other end of the phone insisted.

"Let me call you back. I'ma go ahead and call her again on her cell phone." I leaned back in the black swivel desk chair—took a deep blank mental exhale, before I made the call. I was disappointed that I was not going to be able to go out.

But, I was more so feeling a touch of shittyness and sense of being disrespected as I looked at the clock on the microwave, then on the stove, on the phone.

I was paranoid, because I know damn well none of these clocks had second hands on it. But, yet, it in slow motion was tick-tocking away in my peripheral vision. They read in 3-D, 12:27 and 39seconds.

An unfamiliar rap song came on, then the automated announcer stating to leave a message after the tone or to press 5 to leave a call back number. I pressed the five. I left the number and I left a few messages: "Hi moms, I was calling to see if you were okay it's late and you were supposed to be here over a hour ago. I haven't heard anything. No one is answering your house phone. You're not answering your cell. None of your contacts are answering. You need to come and pick up your daughter. I hope you're okay."

The other messages were shorter, pretty much someone need to pick up the little girl. At some point one would say just go to bed and contact someone in the morning. My insides was having an anxiety attack—please. I reflected on the amount of time I've cared for this little girl. She was one month and half away from her fourth birthday. She was four months when she started. I always dealt with the grandmother. She was the one paying me, picking up and dropping off, even when the mother signed up and qualified and received the county vouchers.

She was picking up at ten o'clock in the evening. Always on time. She informed me that she was no longer going to be picking up her granddaughter. That, she'd just be dropping her off for the next few weeks. Then, she'd no longer be doing that either. According to her, her daughter was lazy and irresponsible and that she was going to take care of her own child. She was tired and I was tired of waiting for this got-damn fool.

Her contract stated that she'd pick up by eleven twenty. Although, the county give you that one hour traveling time before and after pick-up and drop-off. I personally don't play that shit, especially when the parent works in the area and drives. If they're a ten, fifteen minute drive away, they have thirty minutes. The hell with that grace period. Can't allow that on second shift.

If you have time to go and pick up other people, that means you got off early enough to come and pick up your child. I shouldn't have to wait for you to go and pick up kids, your weed, your dude, nor your grocery.

This particular mother would get to my house no later than eleven twenty on occasions, having several males in the car, maybe little cousins, and neighbors, whomever. At times she'd tell me that she just came from Wal-Mart. On other days she had to have gone to see the dope man, since her and the weed smell got out the car at the same time and knocked on the door.

When I asked who is it, they both answered. Then I'd have to wait before I let the little girl leave, until the car aired out and give my little lecture.

The point is that she got off sooner and earlier than she told those county workers—who tells you that sometimes the parents need a break away from their kids. We don't get paid for breaks.

See these workers are the ones putting this bull in their heads. Having them think that they got it like that. This mother and others would come to me or call me to ask if they could drop off early. They have a doctor's appointment before they go to work.

What the f* * *!, does that have to do with me. Then, you're suppose to be professional and reserved at all times. How professional could you make this statement: "You simple minded-illiterate-lazy-pompous ass-frazzled-dazzled-fickled-silly ass beyatch. You better come and get your got-damn kids, children on time." You can't sound professional with that. Nor did I at 1:17 in the got damn morning.

I sat on the covered cream sofa. My arm not relaxed on the arm of it, but, it's there—as I massage my eyelids. The little girl is a dear. But, she's unusually louder than anyone I know. That's not true, she's louder than any other child that I've met, but, as loud as an obnoxious loud adult. I was bothered that she was up. I tried to get them up and ready during second shift thirty minutes before pickup.

She was up and ready by eleven o'clock. I'm expecting her to be gone in twenty minutes. Her mom didn't show up at her regular time. Okay she's running late. The little girl can't go to sleep. Her mother should be coming at anytime. I'm still not letting her lie back down. It's midnight and I know she should be coming around the corner—knocking on the door any second. But, she didn't.

I don't know what's going on. She's not answering her phone. I left a message earlier—called several times—paged her on her cell phone.

Now her mailbox is full, not by me, but, it's full. On top of that, her phone was ringing several times before her voice mail picked up. Suddenly, as the evening ends and the late morning hours of Saturday morning arrives, her voice mail picks up instantly.

Meantime, her daughter is still up, loud as ever—demanding. I told her to get a pillow until her mother comes. She's even louder because she doesn't want to. I didn't want her to go to sleep, because I wasn't picking her big ass up. She was tall for her age and thick. She spoke very well. From her speaking and height you would have thought she was entering first grade.

"Miss. Peggy, I want some cookies."

"No. Sit down and relax until it's time to go."

"May I have a banana and chips?"

"I said no. Stop asking me."

"It's Friday. I want my snacks." she whimpered. She is so freaking loud now. It's ridiculous. She's not crying, just whining—loudly.

Her voice doesn't have much baby tone to it. Certain words. Other than that, loud. She's woken up my kids, who's downstairs in my face.

"Why is she still her mommy?"

"Did you call her mother or grandmother?"

"I can't wait till you stop doing daycare, ugh!"

"You better charge them a late fee too, mommy."

Now, I have three kids.

Two in which are back to back in age—teen girls. They're simultaneously saying this to me, as they're telling the little girl to be quiet. Who's asking them for snacks because it's Friday, or could she have some chicken, rice, macaroni and cheese or a peanut butter sandwich. We saw a bright light entering into the house, from the side window, that was covered by gray and black scalloped valances.

"It's about time!" one of my daughters stated, as she looked out of one of the rectangle block windows on the front door to be sure. "Ooh, mommy she don't even have on her work clothes."

I leaned back on the black swivel office chair that sat in the middle of the floor, instead of at the computer table. They all were bothering my nerves. Making me have an anxiety attack.

Around this time I suppose to be in tune with myself. Free from any stresses from my work week. Instead, I'm trying to collect my composure, to make sure that I present myself in an easy delicate professional manner.

I walk across the gray carpeted floor. I open up the door and the screen door, her child is behind me, my kids went back upstairs. The crisp cold breeze of a late April night hit me. I didn't feel it. I was boiling. Before I could say anything or get on the porch good enough she opened her freaking mouth. I held my composure as long as I could.

"I know . . . I'm late . . . I'm not tryin' to hear you . . . I—she cut her sentence short. Waving her arms everywhere—like she was trying to land an aircraft, as she walked towards the front porch.

"So you're okay and everything's alright?"

"No everything is . . . not okay." She angrily punched in her hands as she made the statement. "And, I'm not about to get into wit chew either."

"You're going to have to tell me something. You're going to have to give me a reason-"

"Hold up Miss. Peggy. I ain't got to tell you a damn thing. This my business. I ain't got to tell you nothing, if I don't want to. And, I ain't about to." I gently smiled. Facilitating a front. Inside I was telling her off.

"Okay. Listen. You were supposed to be here a long time ago. I've called, left messages and called your job—with no prevail."

"I found out who been breaking into my house. Who probably be the same muthafuckas that stole my car! I had to clean up and shit! I ain't go to work. I had to take care of some business, me and my dude."

"You were there?! They caught them?"

"Naw, they betta be lucky I wasn't."

"Did the police take any finger prints, or anything?" I didn't give a damn. I'm just running, the usual lying suspect—let me catch her in a lie routine. Oh don't get me wrong, it's sad day in the neighborhood. Sorry that it happened. It's late. I don't care.

"This happened a couple of days ago."

I began to smile as I was trying to keep my inner egos in check.

There was a slight sigh.

"This is remarkable. Um, you're going to have to pay a late fee, due immediately. It's unfortunate what happened to you. But, it has nothing to do with me, my family or my business. Then, you tell me that you didn't even go to work. Yet, you come hours late to pick up your-"

"Hold up, hold up. I'm glad I didn't go to work. I found out some things, paid some bills and took care of my house. Yo job is to stay in the house and keep them little muthafuckas." She stormed.

"Don't call them that."

"Well, hey, shit."

The little girl, thank goodness, went and got into the car. Just in a nick of time. Someone was coming to shut this scene down.

"My job is to keep you guys kids, while you go to work or to school. For no other reason should I be keeping your child, unless I agree. I have bills to pay just like you."

"Last time I checked you can pay them at the corner store."

"Why should I have to pay my bills at the corner store? Just like you had a choice where and when you were going to pay your bills, I supposed to have that same choice. I can't do that if you guys don't pick up your kids."

"Shiied, get them bad little muthafuckas—take them to the corner store and pay yo bills. Or, you can take that shit to the mailbox and mail it off. They pick up bills, too. This the job you chose. That's yo choice. Don't-

"What time is it?"

"After one. So . . . so what. What that shi-

"Let me tell you something. Don't you ever come on this here property at no time talking to me like that. I'm professional during business hours. This—don't count as one of those hours. Yes, I chose this position. I choose when I start work and get off of work—not you or no one else.

If you have something other than school or work to do, then, you do it with your child. I don't give a damn what you had to do, who you caught, where you had to be. I don't give a damn, if you were in cardiac arrest.

Unless you called me, you better had been in the back of that EMS truck with your daughter. She better had been rolling down the street in the back seat of your mama's car. But, by no means, don't you ever get it twisted that this is my world, that your child is my all day responsibility, my struggle. No the hell it's not and she's not.

You need childcare. I don't. I can have you replaced, by the time you get into your car. That's all you are, is a slot—in reality. Not my responsibility. I love your daughter, love her. Love don't run shit here. You understand.

You take your child to the damn corner store and pay your bills. You take your child to your appointments, so that she could scream and act up—with you, her mother. I don't have to go through that shit. The next time you come on this . . . here property, you better come correct or don't come at all. 'Cause you'll get you're feeling hurt here!

Was that professional? Hell no. Was I trying to be professional? Hell not! Yes, I said it, hell not. I couldn't be professional at one in the morning.

She stood there just staring in ultimate shock. See, I'm always smiling—always got that ear and shoulder for someone. I never came undone. Not in front of my clients. I can't recall—nope never. I don't use slang around or during daycare hours, nor can anyone else.

Then, she's going to act as if all is okay—asking me if I could answer her phone to let her new boyfriend, old boyfriend know that she's still at my house. Since, he's not going to believe her.

She finished out the remaining weeks. And, never returned until several months later. Her mother saw me in Tops Grocery store and waved me down, tripping over herself.

"Miss. Peggy, I'm so glad I ran into you. I was hoping I did," she nonchalantly giggled.

"How are you and everyone else?"

"Everybody's doing good. I know you and my daughter had a falling out. She said she'll apologize."

"Aw, don't worry about it."

"No, she's gone apologize. I'ma start keeping her daughter again and I need your help. Please, say she can come back to yo daycare."

"I don't have a problem with her coming back. I just don't want to have to deal with your daughter. I don't do the young mothers, no."

"I'll be dropping her off and picking her up."

She did just that, for like a month and a half. Her daughter dropped off one afternoon, standing at the side door—trying to apologize. I accepted and everything was cool.

She told stories of what was going on in her life, as she always did. They were there (at my daycare) for a long time since their return—for like eight months. Then, April rolled around again. Damn nut lost her mind, yet again.

I saw signs already. I wasn't expecting what was to come. I saw some unsteadiness with her performance. She stopped picking up herself. She rarely dropped off. She informed me that she had a new roommate, who would be dropping off and picking up. Come to find out it was a dude she met off the street—known less than a month.

Then, I received a list of individuals that would be picking her daughter up. The first list was like nine different guys and maybe a female. I informed her that they would have to be on her contract. She had a problem with that. It's her daughter. She felt whomever she chose to pick up her child is her choice. She was right.

Not trying to be right or wrong—I was right in not agreeing for that type of traffic to take place at my facility, my home.

More people were added on it (the list). This arose a month and a half before the last incident. See, a couple of my rules are: anyone other than the parent picking up or dropping off must show I.D., which the information is copied. Another rule is that: anyone other than the parent picking up, must pick up two hours before the child's scheduled pick up time.

Now those rules were for security purposes. Especially, the two hour in advance pick-up rule. If the parents' chosen person didn't pick up on time, that would have given me enough time to contact the parent to make other arrangements for pick up.

It also wouldn't had interfered with my personal time, right. If the parent supposed to pick up at eleven and the person she/he chose to pick up instead, had to pick up by nine. But, I think my second shift was always a eight o'clock pick up, if they weren't on the parent and provider agreement—even still.

It was becoming a problem for her. All of these different people had become a problem for me. And it was sort of dangerous—to me. I was trying to hold out until the little girls fifth birthday, before I let her go. Hell, she was about to start school in a few months, anyway. Maybe, I'd try to hold out until then.

No, it wouldn't be able to get that far.

I had her since she was like four months, I believe. So, we all wanted to throw her a big party. Give her some gifts, school supplies, uniforms, outfits, toys etc. We wanted to see her off in a big stylish way. It didn't work out that way.

"Hello, who is this again? Oh, wow. Weren't you supposed to call, yesterday at the latest, to let me know that you weren't coming today? Jeez, you could have called this morning. It's like dinner time." She laughed on the phone.

"My bag, Miss. Peggy, I know. But, I got to get straight to the point. Did you get my message?"

"Miss. Peggy, do you think that, you could wave my co-pay for this month? Please call me back as soon as possible—with a yes or no. I'll really appreciate it. I know she missed some days and it's gone hurt me to have to pay $160. And, she's been there for less than two whole weeks. Even if you can't, it won't be a big deal, thanks Miss. Peggy."

"Yeees. I left a message—"

"Yeah, I . . . got . . . that message. But, I don't understand. You did it before and it wasn't no problem. So, what's the problem now?"

"It's not a problem. It's just that, I said I'm not going to be able to do it."

"Well, what I gotta pay?"

"You have to pay whatever your co-pay is? So, what is it? I know that you went to your re-determ' yesterday. So, whatever it is, bring it in with your new placement letter."

"I told you, it's $160 now and they didn't switch my hours. And, I don't see why come I have to pay all of that money. Can I pay half or something'? Shit, she ain't been there, like that."

"I don't know what-"

"Miss. Peggy! Are you about to tell me you can't help me?"

"Look, the rule is the rule. I'm sorry."

"Miss. Peggy, she missed days. Why do I have to pay for her not being there?"

"She missed three days. Today will be the fourth. You supposed to pay on the first day of the month, for your portion of the voucher. You don't get prorated because you're choosing to keep her out to avoid paying; if that's what you're doing. We're two weeks and a day into the month. We have two and a half to go. It's five weeks in this month."

"You tryin' to tell me you can't help me this one month—when she don't even stay all day at yo' daycare? My placement letter says, she supposed to be there from two to twelve midnight. You let me bring her over early, if I ask. Then, you tell me she has to be picked up early.

So, you telling me that I have to pay you. And, welfare paying for hours she don't supposed to be there and hours that I have on my placement letter that you don't even keep her. I'ma call my worker and ask her about that. That's wuss up.

I know what you could do? I can keep her home and my brother can keep her until my friend gets off of work. And, you could just keep the voucher and give me half of that money. Shit, I'm tryin' to come up too."

"I'm amazed. I'm in utter amazement. I don't—"

"I ain't into how you feelin' I want to know if you gone hook me up or not. Shit, I even got a cousin who'll keep her. All I have to do is give her something to drink and a pack of cigarettes. That's all she wants.

But, if she want some money, I'd give her ten, twenty dollars, that ain't shit. Long as you givin' me some money. I'ma call my worker to see how much those vouchers worth. And, we gone split that."

We address one another at my daycare with a Miss or Mister in front of the first name. So, that's how I addressed her. But, usually I say, moms or dad for my daycare kids sake.

"Miss.—I could go get the number out of your file if you don't have it on hand at this minute. We could discuss this over with her, concerning your hours. They're not responsible for paying for those extra hours. As long as I'm keeping your child during the specified times on your placement letter . . . I'll get paid. This is my business. I have the choice of extending my hours, as long as I'm not over my capacity. I'm not nor have I ever been-"

"Miss. Peggy you full of shit! Tryin' to be professional—talking to me like I'm dumb."

"I don't mean too. But, you're going to have to try to watch how you address me. I'm not concern about you contacting anyone about my hours that I choose to work.

You're welcome to write a complaint that I can put in your file. And, I don't flip vouchers."

"Fuck that. You full of shit, Miss. Peggy. **HOW . . . THE . . . FUCK YOU GONE SAY YOU DON'T FLIP VOUCHERS, YOU OFFERED ME A HUNDRED DOLLARS WHEN I FIRST GOT THE VOUCHERS!? PEOPLE SAID I SHOULDA LET JO MUTHAFUCKIN' ASS GO A LONG TIME AGO!"**

"Wait a minute . . . wait, wait. What time is it?"

"I know what fuckin' time it is."

I just giggled to myself.

"I want to make sure we on the same time, 'cause we're definitely not on the same page."

"It's six forty-five, I know you off."

"Right, and I'm not on the clock."

"What that supposed to mean? This business and it's gone be handled today."

"Business that's gone be handled to . . . night." I got that off of Bernie Mack—to . . . night. It's funny to me.

"I don't know who the freak you think I am, or what I am. Let me reassure you, I'm far from anything that you can imagine. Don't call me with that dumb shit. I don't flip vouchers. I offered you the hundred dollars, becausc you paid for a week, that, the county approved.

So, I refunded your money. As far as your stupid, ignorant ass friends, I don't give a damn about them. You hollering because I won't do anything illegal with your ass. Send her somewhere else because I won't get dirty with you.

Did your daughter know her alphabets, numbers and shapes, by time she turned two?"

"Yeah."

"Was your daughter able to recognize and point out and tell every number, letter and shape and certain words at three years old?"

"Yeah."

"Your daughter speaks in complete sentences, know your information, along with her own. She's writing. She can read. She's doing more than any one of your friends' kids are doing—hell more than your average kindergartener does. Right or wrong?" "I mean yeah, but-"

"There's no but. I told you I don't need you. You need me. You need us. You need someone to keep your child. I run a business. I don't have time for no bull. I replace people if I have too. Before I hang up this phone, you'll be replaced. Call your friends, your peeps, whom ever. You burned your bridge, here."

Several months later I got a message from her mother—asking me to call her as soon as I got a chance.

THE END LITERALLY

Another reason this book is being written, is because someone has to speak up for the individuals who are keeping other people children. Someone has to open up the door, to let others see inside of daycare. No matter how much childcare or any field dealing with the care of a child is minimized, it's the most highly intricate, encumbrance, rewarding position to possess—other than being a parent.

It's more ferocious, due to, the handicap of not knowing the many different characters, problems, situations, the psyche of these grown ass people and these little growing minds, that's entering into your space, your life, your home when you're doing childcare from home.

Does the facilities, centers, buildings, churches get this side of the business, perhaps on a mediocre stage of it. I think it's more inconsequential—with no disrespect intended. They keep up a façade. Every now and then they (parents) may show their ass. They're more into the public eye. So, they're a little more cautious, than, when they're attending a childcare business ran from a residential property.

They expect more, from home childcare providers. They think one has access to much more, by working from home. Seemingly, home childcare providers are expected to do more, from sort of threat of losing their clientele if they don't. Although, I may have stated that I think that, 'Others', situations with these families are trivial. Yet, in contradiction, they're still poignant. They get a respect that home childcare providers don't. We have to take and demand more so, should I say.

Provider: Good Morning. Give me some sugar. The provider teases the two children coming into her house for childcare, hugging and kissing their cheeks, then suddenly pauses.

Unt, un, you have to clean their faces and noses. That's disgusting.

Parent1: Oh, I thought I cleaned their faces.

Provider: Hi, what are you eating. I want some, the provider teases the little girl. What is this all over her? She asked about the many different stains that didn't go with what she was eating. Especially sense it was balled up and wrinkled.

Parent2: She has another shirt in her bag.

Provider: Well you have to bring her back in with a clean shirt on.

You can't drop her off no where looking like that.

Parent3: Excuse me, she said to the parent exiting. Good Morning. Somebody left you a present.

Provider: Hello, ugh, what's that?

Parent3: I told you somebody left you a gift. He just did it. So, I guess he wanted you to change him.

Provider: No. No . . . you need to take him back out and bring him back in with a fresh pamper on. The provider said as she closed her eyes and walked away.

Parents: I was rushing cause you be on it, with that breakfast. You don't give nobody time to get here. "I know. When she says breakfast is over it's over. Ain't nobody got time for all of that." The third parent mumbles under her breath. Yet, loud enough for the provider standing close by to hear, but, no one else.

Provider: I have a schedule, just like any other facility. So, I don't know what you all are trying to say. I'm running a business, sorry. *Wake your lazy asses up and get off your backs you'll have time to feed your own kids.*

PHASE THREE

LET'S EAT

I hope I'm not considered a modern day mother. That'll be embarrassing. In contradiction, when it comes to my clients, I want them to view me as a modern day caregiver. I'm-not-cooking jack! I mean I do. I don't want them to know that. Banquets, Tyson's, hot pockets, pot pies will be defrost in a minute. I don't see nothing wrong with it.

That's another reason I'm not keen on the food program, good idea, nice program, but, it's not for me. I signed up for it before. The worker was going over the expectations with me. When I learned that all foods must be fresh. That's wasteful. It's an inconvenience. Other centers and schools are reimbursed under a food program in which they don't serve fresh foods. Well, I don't think they do.

I don't serve fresh foods to my family like that, perhaps fruits. But, their meals aren't cooked from fresh produce, daily. I'd teach the kids some fundamentals. I'm no Betty Crocker. I know that I'm not the only non Betty Crocker, biscuit baking, pea snapping, oven mitten wearing provider. Hell, the parents don't do all of that.

You know what, this is one of the biggest problems there is in childcare. It's not the money (in hindsight, it is) it's not the families inconsiderate, malevolent, inconsistent.

I'm . . . so . . . willing . . . to . . . help you with my kids growth mannerism.

It is truly, without a doubt what out weighs all situations—it's meal time. You could request from the parent that they work with you to help their own child with their curriculum, their response will be; "Okay. Did they eat? What they eat?" This is about to be an explosive situation with childcare providers—with the economy the way it is-explosive. This is what's going to be eliminated in households; meals. People are going to consider their children having a sufficient amount of food for the day, coming from school, childcare, or wherever they child goes.

EXCERPTS FROM WHO'S KEEPING YOUR CHILDREN?

O.K., What about the meals? Did you ever tell your families, that your meals are served at a certain time. That, if they're not there at your facility at that time the child would not be fed.

Did you ever have to tell your families, that, their child would only be fed certain meals. But, they always try to either show up too early or too late, just so their child could be fed, anyway.

Now I use to do just that, if a child was in my house when it was time for dinner, even if they were soon to leave in minutes, I fed them. Please, I won't do it again.

Why wouldn't I? 'Cause, I won't. My responsibility has to end at some point. Our responsibilities as childcare providers has to end.

Those kids have parents or guardians that drops them off and someone picks them up. They're to take on their obligations of tending to the needs of those kids. But, ah, naw, we have some new breeders in town.

"Did you guys eat?"

"We had an apple, some milk and a cookie."

"Oh, okay. Well go sit down so that you all can do your work."

"Work, we not going to eat breakfast first?"

"Breakfast, didn't you say you had an apple, cookie and some milk?"

"Yeah, but, that's not no breakfast. We hungry. My mom said we were going to eat breakfast over hear."

"Breakfast here was over with twenty minutes ago."

Was it wrong, I mean not giving them something else to eat?

I remember watching Judge Joe Brown, one day. I always try to watch one of the court shows when it's pertaining to childcare. They're insightful. You learn a lot. Being wiser from the knowledge of others situations, makes you keener on how to regulate your own business. It had something to do with a provider suing a parent for unpaid fees. The parent went on and on, about this and that, why she shouldn't have to pay the fees.

To me she didn't have a leg to stand on, but, I guess you have to listen to everything, even if it's nonsense. One of her excuses for not wanting to pay is that, the provider wouldn't feed her daughter anything, when she dropped her off. The provider informed Judge Joe Brown, that, breakfast was over with. She went on to enlighten him on the fact that, the mother was over two hours late. The mother interrupted to state that she bought a pack of oatmeal for the provider to cook, who refused to do so.

He kind of got to me. He responded with his, I don't tolerate that tone of voice. Quote, unquote—"Why may I ask, you couldn't take the time out to give her some breakfast?"

Respect my business. My business comes with rules and regulations, schedules and timelines—deadlines, deadlines. People are already under the impression, that, the providers working from home is not doing anything. Therefore, they should act like they're on fire and stop, drop and roll for one of them. No, not I.

Nor am I going to hop around like some damn kangaroo—for no one—your child, your responsibility. Paula Dean works on the food network, she does not live in my house, never been in my kitchen. Oh, yes she has, the day I had that thirteen inch t.v. in my kitchen.

We as providers take on temporary situations. At no point should these situations turn into problems. The temporary situations is this: you have to go to school, a training program, another job, 'cause your first job is being a parent to your own kids. At all times you're on call—we'll keep and care for your child.

Just follow the rules, timeline, the deadline and make sure we're paid. Whatever it is that you have to do—do. This is how and what you need to accommodate yourself. That's just a temporary situation for us. This is not an adoption agency. This is not a soup kitchen, no disrespect to anyone.

This is a profession in which someone needs temporary relief for childcare assistance. Mealtime and snack time is a part of that. At no time should it become a problem or a struggle for any provider.

STORY TIME

ALL IN A WEEKS WORK

"Wake up bay."

"Why? It looks like it's still dark outside."

"Right. It is." Adrianna said with laughter.

"Damn, you horny baby? You want daddy?" Faizon said with a little cockiness, but, was quickly soften.

"No."

"Aw, it's like that."

"No, I told you, you have to be up and gone early. I work today." Adrianna laughed out her words.

"Damn baby, you making me feel like you don't won't me around. What's wrong with me being here?"

"It's nothing wrong with you being here, as long as it's not during my daycare hours. It's, it's just business."

"What if we lived together—you gone tell me to leave then, too."
"I'm not worried about anything like that." Faizon curiously stared at Adrianna, who read his puzzling expression.

"Look, you're a man and the first thing these people would say if they can't have their way, or if they need a scapegoat for some mess that happened in their lives, is to blame it on someone at daycare. The man that's there. So . . . to avoid all of that . . . I give them no open opportunity."

"I don't know how this is going to work. You seem like you hiding something or you don't trust me."

"Don't be like that. That's not fair."

"You always telling me to leave or I can't eat this or that, because it's daycare food. You got more food for them, than you have for your own family. I can't call during certain hours. You don't answer during certain hours. I can't take my woman out because she never get off on time. And, when you do go out with me, you want to leave early, cause you got to get up early.

How is this gone possibly work?" Tell me. Faizon questioned as he finally hyped himself up and set on the edge of the bed to get dress, without even freshening up as he usually does.

"It's a business, Fay. I mean, you can't take me to your job. I don't know what to say. I don't know what you want me to do. You're welcome to eat whatever you want. I like hanging out with you. You can call me anytime on my cell phone, but, at my house during certain hours, it's a business line. I don't always want to answer."

"Can you fix me some breakfast?"

"What do you want?"

"I saw some breakfast burritos. Can I have a couple?" Adrianna bit the back of her hands. Raising from the opposite side of the bed to go answer the phone that began to ring.

The answering service intercepted her gesture to avoid his request.

One of her parents was leaving a message asking permission to drop her children off a little early.

"Um, umm, those are for daycare."

"Man, I'm about to go. I'm good." The phone continued to ring. Another message was left. Adrianna continued to ignore it. She walked Faizon out to his car. He didn't kiss her as it was normal for him to do so. He put one hand on her shoulder, as she was opened armed to hug him.

"I'll call you. No, you call me, when you get permission from yo' daycare peeps."

"Come on. Don't do that. Call me okay."

"I'll holla at chew. I got things to do. Ain't no hard feelings, just business." She watched him drive away as the brittle rain drops of the early fall morning began to fall down. She turned to step inside of the house, just to hear the phone ringing again. She cursed at the person on the other end of that call, in her head.

After washing up and doing her hair, along with straightening up the house. Adrianna was preparing for the beginning of the Monday morning work week. It was now going on eight o'clock in the morning. The parent that was calling all morning haven't even arrived yet.

She was due at seven o'clock. Assuming she wasn't coming, she prepared breakfast for the family that was now expected to arrive. Adrianna cut up construction papers for the kids projects.

The toddler tables were set. Although it was cold outside, she had the back door open. So, that, the floor could dry up quickly as she finished up mopping. Five minutes later, the door opens and the two little ones come barging through, with a handful of dirty leaves and muddy shoes. The mother enters with her infant in her arms. "How you doing? Get over here and throw the leaves outside." Adrianna requested from the little ones—whose mother could care less. Considering, she said nothing before. But said a lot with her facial expression of a—who you think you are! She turned her back as she exited shaking her head.

"See y'all later. See you Ms. Seffron."

"Okay, see you later. Come over here, let me see your bags."

"Why you taking my leaffesses?" one child said, while the other said that their mommy said put it in the bag. Adrianna did not care. She knew that it was only a matter of time that they would pull those leaves out of their bags and make a mess.

While in the process of throwing the leaves in the outside trash, she heard the next family arriving.

“Get over here, before I pop your little ass!”

“No! no!”

“You’ll get it, when I pick you up later. Now stop it, before you get it.”

Adrianna was beginning to go towards the family and decided against it. She hated when some of her clients, would give there preschoolers a sippy cup, all the way up to getting to her house then would take it away, knowing they were going to have a temper tantrum. And, a temper tantrum is exactly what the three and a half year old had.

The mother signed him in and left. He set off the ripple effect. The other kids started to cry. The infant as if someone had hurt her. It was easy to get the other two to calm down.

“He’s okay. Stop crying and eat your food. Breakfast is over. I’m about to clean up. If you don’t eat, I’m throwing it away. So, let’s eat, hmm, yummy.”

The little boy also stop crying and came to sit in his chair. Suddenly, he flipped the plate containing a pancake and a side of strawberry flavored applesauce on the floor. He was upset that his childcare provider had given him a cup (not his sippy cup) of milk which also went spilling on the floor.

The kids were now calm. They were doing their work. The day had calmed itself, for the moment. Just then, it was a knock on the door.

Adrianna had taken a deep breathe. The parent that had called earlier was now arriving three hours later according to the time that they were supposed to arrive—five hours later from the what seem to have been a desperate need for early care.

Adrianna said nothing of the call, but, had to say something about the lateness, since the mother felt the need to complain about snack time.

"Oh, what is that they're about to eat?"

"Um, a peanut butter and jelly bar and a cup of milk."

"My kids didn't eat, breakfast. They need more than that."

"Well, it's snack time. This is a snack."

"Don't my co-pay pays for more than a graham cracker snack time?"

"Look, it's too early for all of this. I don't know what you want. What it is, that you need from me. I have to take care of business."

"Oh, I just want to know for now, what are you doing with my money, that, I give to you every month? It seems like you're neglecting—She was interrupted by Ms. Sheffron.

"Look, I don't know what's going on with you today. But, let me reassure you that, no child is neglected here. You pay for childcare and that's it. And, you don't pay for that. You barely pay a quarter of the total bill. You need to talk to your worker and ask them the purpose of a co-pay." Adrianna said as she put the infant girl in the playpen.

"I'm asking you, Ms. Sheffron. You supposed to be the childcare provider. You the one I suppose to come to when I have concern with the care you provide."

"What is your concern? I'm sorry."

"I asked you, already. My kids didn't eat breakfast. You just want to give them some crackers. Then on top of that, I called to see if I could drop off early and you didn't answer, nor called back. That's unprofessional. Had I known that you weren't going to feed them, I could have fix them something to eat myself or asked somebody else to keep them."

"Stupid ass, bitch, that's what you should had done anyway. You had them. You lazy hoe. Ugh! I can't stand these stupid ass people. Oh, I wish I could just tell them all, take you're stankin' asses home and raise your own kids." Adrianna thought to herself.

"Look, it's obvious, that, you're bothered this morning. But, this is not the place for all of that. Ok. If you want to take your kids back home with you—ok. They're your kids. Besides, they're not suppose to be here, if you're not working. You know that right?"

"How you know what I have to do?"

The kids were up running around, making a mess. Adrianna was irritated. The mother was antsy about getting back at her provider for not answering the phone during the early morning hours. Hours, that, she wasn't even qualified for, nor was childcare hours available for those hours.

"Look, you supposed to be at work by eight o'clock. It's practically eleven. So . . .

"Maybe, I have to work this afternoon." she interrupted.

"It's fine. Umm, today will have to be the last day that they come here for childcare, when you don't have to work. You have vouchers and a contract that states your work hours. Also, your job doesn't have second shift.

If the county or the state find out that I kept your kids and you didn't work, I'll get in trouble for that. Because they don't pay on those days. And, I'm not paying nothing back. But, you go ahead and have a nice day. Please read your contract, because this is stated in it.

By the way, this is my business during 7am thru 12 midnight. That's when I clock in and out. If you're calling to say anything, then, that's when you call. Even then, I don't answer my phone unless it's one of my parents for that shift.

I assume anyone calling at a later time then their shift, is calling to inform me of a day they're not showing up or they're going to be late. I don't mean to be an inconvenience, but, like other businesses there has to be a cut off time of operations.

As the week moved along, Adrianna finds herself in a small rut. The check was not in the mail. Everyone is hungry and must eat. The ones that will have to be sacrificed would be her family.

"Mom, why we can't have a can of ravioli, or hot dogs?"

"I didn't get paid, yet. I have to let this food stretch and make sure I have enough to feed the daycare kids."

"Daycare—what about us, mom?"

"You two are teens. You-will-survive. Besides, I'm going to make a big pot of spaghetti, or beans and muffins. It should last a couple of days. If I don't get paid by then, I'll make another pot of something."

"Why they can't eat it, too?"

"I didn't—be quiet." She said with irritation.

There was a knock at the door. A smile came across her face. It was him—Faizon. She was missing him. But, the smile quickly disappeared when she glanced at the time. It was after six. He's just getting off of work. She rolled her eyes in her head. She said to herself; *go home. I don't have any food to feed you. Everybody damn hungry.*

Enough is never enough. She raked her hands through her hair; laid up against the salmon painted walls; trying not to come undone with anger, tears, regret and defeat. She can't get through the week or next week without some sort of pay.

That meal fed to Faizon, had cost her. That one little meal.

Of course, he wanted seconds. And, yes her kids wanted to try some wild rice, flank steaks, with sauteed onions and gravy, garlic, buttery asparagus and flaky layered biscuits.

She had to pay her bills. She's now waiting for two paychecks. Miss. Sheffron had the audacity to ask her man for fifty bucks. "You want me to pay for eating here?" He asked puzzlingly.

"I didn't get paid. I need to take care of some business. Don't worry, I'll give it right back to you, as soon as I get paid."

"Look, sweetheart, I'm not worried about you repaying me. I'm considering why suddenly, you're asking me for money. You never did before. Why do you need it?" He asked suspiciously.

"I have to get food for my daycare kids."

"I can't do it. You are making me pay for eating a damn meal! You didn't say you needed it for your kids or for bills, shit—not even just to have it, just in case. You want it for someone else responsibility."

"Fay what is wrong with asking the man that's a part of my life, if he can help me out?"

"'Cause at this moment, I can't be your man." He stood up from the hunter green, soft Italian, leather sofa. His condescending demeanor and facetious reaction took Adrianna by shock. She had a pause in her; what the—, as she witness her man of one year and a half, smug departure from her life.

In the back of her mind, since the moment they became intimate and he visited her at her house, she felt he walked with green eyes. And now, all is official.

He stood tall as he straightened his collar, fixed his cuffs and checked his well groomed face, in the mirrored back picture frame, which displayed Adrianna in one of her finest moments. She was in a white silk, diamond strapped, low cut gown, with a high slit on the side—leaning against the boulder rocks at the lake, looking towards the sunset.

With a twitch in his neck and raise in his brow, he began to insinuate.

"I come over here, I can't go in that room. I can't sit there. I want to take my lady out for a nice time, I can't do that. You have to get home early to prepare for, according to you, your business. I try to buy you nice things—you don't except it. You claim you have it all of the—

"You must be out of your mind. Here I am trying keep my business afloat, while you're trying to drown me with this sorrowful nonsense. Fifty dollars you can keep. How can you be upset because I'm letting you know ahead of time, before you spend your money up on something, that I already have?

Furthermore, you can sit and hang out wherever you choose to in my house, except for my kids room. On top of that, I don't even know why you would want to, or complain about hanging in rooms that I myself don't even hang out in.

What's the purpose of buying nice things if everyone is going to treat as if it was frivolously bought. She rhetorically asked. What are you acting piqued for?"

As if she never said a word, he continued.

"You claim you have it all suddenly. You have pictures of everybody, somewhere, everywhere in this house. I was with you when you took this pic'. Somehow I'm not in it with you."

He turned to face her. He released a sigh of accomplishment.

"You embarrassed of me, Miss. Sheffron? Are you? I knew one day you was going to need me. Here we are. You walked around here like you were better than me. You a babysitter. That's not an accomplishment. You can't even feed them."

Adrianna let him go on and on with his insecurities of ranting and raving. She knew he was looking for his moment to gloat. A woman who had a lucrative home daycare business, a nice piece of property and accessories to trim, was an intimidation for him. But, right then, her neediness for that fifty dollars, was his right of passage to being a wanted man.

He tried to give her the money, plus one—with an apology. But, his right of passage to becoming a wanted man, was his passage out of Adrianna's life. He wasn't needed.

She realized that he became so unnecessarily irked over nothing, that he revealed envious and jealous behavior towards her independency. She didn't trust that behavior nor the unforeseen future reactions, around herself nor her daughters who also mentioned that night (after she asked Faizon to leave) they wanted to stay over to their grandparents for a little while. They felt that the business was coming before them.

UNTIL TOMORROW THE END

There's no room for the toleration, of someone believing that we as childcare givers are solely responsible for every meal a child is nourished with and not the parent/guardian.

A child would never remember breaking bread with his or her own mother or father, if the child were always expected to eat with someone else's family.

"Mom, where's their mother?"

"Whose mother?"

"Those two right there."

"Why?"

"I just wanted to know?"

"Don't play mind games with me. You didn't just walk in here from school, not saying hi—asking me about somebody else's mother."

"I was just asking. I saw their mother and father at home on our way home from school."

"I don't care. They paid me. It's none of my business."

Now the mother and father is like twenty or more minutes late. There is a late fee to consider. You would think it'll be a concern.

"Oh, hi."

"Sorry we're running late."

"Aw, that's . . . where you guys coming from?"

"Well, I took him . . . well we went out to dinner, together."

"That's nice. What are you guys and the kids going to eat? I know you bought a good doggie bag home."

"Huh, did you want something to eat? The mother asked neither one of children in particular, considering they were running up and down the driveway. I'll find you something when we get home."

What kind of mess was that?

"They didn't eat?"

"Not dinner."

"Humm, they weren't hungry."

"I don't know. I gave them a snack a hour and a half ago."

"AN HOUR AND A HALF AGO! It's dinner time."

"Oh I don't do dinner here. I don't have any kids during dinner hours."

"You should had told me that. I didn't know that."

No, no, if you're suppose to pick up before dinner time, that means you're supposed to have dinner prepared or an idea what they were going to eat at home.

Oh, I'll give them something to eat. Don't call it a meal. Even if I fed the daycare kids a meal, I wouldn't tell the parents.

I am not lying to you when I tell you, that, these people are out for themselves. I truly believe at the end of the day, when it all boils down to the nitty-gritty no one else matters, never has.

They'll pretty much tell you in their own special way—you the provider is responsible for my child in every way. When I pick up her or him, I don't want to have to do nothing but smell my own ass and feed my own big ass mouth.

Parent: "Do you feed them before I pick them up?"

Provider: "Yes, they have meals over here."

Parent: "No, I'm talking about do you feed them dinner? Because, they act like they're starving when they get home."

Provider: "Oh, no. Dinner is served to children scheduled to be here after six o'clock."

Parent: "Well, do they have snacks after they get out of school?

'Cause you talkin' about you don't give them nothing to eat for dinner. Shoot tha . . . tha . . . that's a long time to go with . . . without food. I don't pick them up un . . . until six.

My son eats lunch in school around 11:30, 12:30. I need to know what I have to do when I go home. Do I have to help with homework? Do I have to cook dinner? That's a lot to have to do. I have to kn . . . know, so I can ge . . . ge . . . get my mind right for that."

Now don't get me wrong. I think there's no one in this business, that has a problem with feeding a child. I think the concern is, the parents aren't concern enough with their child.

There's never one child that eats every meal served to them. There's not a child that eats everything on their plate, at every mealtime. I know—I know they can't be served only what they want. Well they won't be served whatever they choose when they're at home, for most kids—depending on their upbringings.

So, why would it be expected somewhere else. As always you know my motto, no child shall eat every meal away from home.

Therefore, the parent should automatically have dinner prepared in advance or be ready to cook when they get home.

Child: "I'm hungry."

Provider: "You can't be that hungry. You didn't eat the oatmeal and you're not just going to eat the bagel. So that you can go through the rest of the morning, saying you're hungry.

Then say the only thing that you had was a bagel.

Child: "But, I didn't eat last night."

Provider: "What does eating oatmeal and a bagel for breakfast here today, have to do with what you ate for dinner, or didn't eat for dinner, yesterday, at home?

Child: "My mom told us that it was too late for us to eat."

Provider: "Too late for you to eat. What time was it?"

Child: "When she woke us up. I don't know what time it was. I think it was about nine or ten at night.

Provider: "Why didn't you eat earlier?

Child: "We had to wait for my mom friend to come over, our auntie. She was coming over for dinner."

Provider: "Well, what time did you fall asleep?"

Child: "At six I think."

Provider: "Why didn't you ask for something to eat? Sunday dinners are usually prepared earlier in the day."

Child: "My mom wasn't finished cooking, yet."

Provider: "What she cook?"

Child: "Ooo, she cooked some yams, some greens, some macaroni and cheese, some chicken and gravy and some other stuff.

Provider: "She cooked all of that and didn't let you guys eat anything?"

Child: "She said it was too late. I'm starving."

Provider: "Well, you still have time to eat your oatmeal and bagel.

Child: "I don't eat oatmeal."

I'm sure providers sympathize with these children. But, how much should a provider carry on their shoulders?

They're your kids. Act like it! We're not playing no damn checkers—you get all of your people on my side, thinking you're king or queen and you're going to wipe me out, puh-leeze. We're not your nanny or your mammy.

No disrespect to the nannies. A nanny is actually, in my opinion close to being a mammy slave. That's derogatory. They can be treated like that at times.

Nannies are expected to be live-in or come early, replacement mothers. While the biological mom is some times right in the same house, at times the same room, the nanny is the one raising and disciplining the child. I know it has to wear on a person, with or without their own child.

I do wonder are nannies rewarded, (other then pay because that's not a reward) with pleasured incentives, vacations, shopping sprees. After all, they are being hired to do the duties of a mother.

I know everyone wants to hope in their beliefs of believing. That you can put your all in all trust in another, but, that'll always be your biggest mistake.

When it comes to your children in the feeding department, you're always to feed your child as if it's the first meal they had for that day.

It'll probably be your (parent) first meal, only meal, in most cases, that, you're preparing for your child/ren for that day, anyway.

You expect the child to eat at school, daycare, preschool or with your hired help. They don't always eat what's served or perhaps just don't eat enough. You can't have a child sit at a table all day waiting for them to decide to eat or finish their meal.

You know what's amazing? When you go to classes, that caters to your extended childcare education and hear people discuss the same thing that you're practically going through or will go through.

It's like you want to ask, have you been spying on me? Do you keep those kids too? Who's their mother?

You always think, it must be you or it must be because of where you live, that these things are occurring.

Okay, some of these things are because of you and where you live. Just be honest with yourself, stop playing.

For the most part it's actually the people who's coming to your place of business, that's bringing all of these different scenarios of what could and will eventually take place.

One of the craziest things that I've notice in my years of doing childcare is, that, we as workers, childcare providers are the excuse to every household problem.

The saddest thing is, it seems as though a persons' biggest problem with their childcare provider is, that, the provider doesn't serve enough food, or meals or doesn't give large enough portions.

Yes, I'm emphasizing on feeding other people children, because they're not emphasizing feeding their own.

There's too many places in this here world, that has many, many people in it with no food. There's many people in these many, many places in this here world who's willing to give their child away hoping someone would adopt their child. Considering, they can't feed their children off a handful of grain. People who would love to sit in front of their family, their children and feed them, watch them eat, are literally dying, because they can't, in other places.

They're traveling miles to bring back just a basket of food. They're stealing, doing anything to get just a meal, something we'll consider just a snack.

Here we are in the United States where you get food tickets, eat for free ticket, yes, foodstamps, WIC, and your kids are hungry. Get the f* * * out of here. They have churches and buildings where you could pick up a couple of bags of food, for free. You telling me these people can't give their kids any food. All of us don't qualify for the program.

Even . . . if . . . I . . . did, I didn't get on the program for someone else's children.

Someone asked me, as I was releasing a little irritation; "But, don't ya'll get paid for this?" I didn't respond. It was stupid to me. Does anyone go to work, for the purpose of supporting others outside of their family? Do you go to work and pick up your paycheck, examine it then say, um, I made five hundred this pay week. I'm going to take majority of this and go by my working or capable neighbors some things that they may like. Come on, Stop it.

No they weren't talking about the food program. They were emphasizing on the amount of a provider's paycheck.

Yes, you suppose to invest in your business. No, your business does not suppose to depend on your everything. If you have to take all that you have, all that's considered—if you have to manipulate your personal finances—subtract from your own children, to give and devote to a business whose basis is not based on food solely, go home. I don't care how old you are, you're not ready. If you're doing more subtracting than you are adding and multiplying, take a nap.

Someone told me that they wouldn't bring their kids to me because I let the daycare kids cry, when they just want more to eat. Told me, that, I was supposed to satisfy their needs. Mom told me this once upon a time, also.

Provider: "How are you doing?"

Parent: "Huh?"

Provider: "I just wanted to know if everything was okay, because I heard through the grapevine, that, you weren't happy with my service. So, I wanted to ask you what were your concerns so, that, I could correct whatever it is for the future?

The provider had already known of the discrepancy from the parents' child.

Parent: "What chew talkin' about? I didn't say nothing. She said, as she gave a sharp stare at her child.

Provider: "Not to get anyone in trouble, I was just told, that, you were looking to transfer your child out of my daycare, because you had a problem with snack time.
Which is fine. I just wanted to know what's the problem, so that I could correct it. I was told it was something about some graham crackers or cheese sandwich."

Parent: "It's not just about no cheese sandwich. I had a problem before I heard about him having six graham cracker sticks and some milk. What kind of snack is that? I have a problem with him telling me he didn't eat a snack when he came to you after school, most of the time."

Provider: "Just so you know, all children get a snack, if they want it. A lot of times your son doesn't want one.

It's not always graham crackers and milk. They're offered fruit cups, fresh fruit, vegetables or veggies and dip, a sandwiches, noodles, things like that, along with something to drink. It's a variety of items, not served in a full portion. It's served as a snack. I don't believe that a snack should be something cooked as a meal. It suppose to be quick.

Also, most of the school age kids bring things back, from school. Which they sometimes trade and eat when they get here. Your son being one of those kids.

He brings things like hot pockets, those peanut butter crustables, yogurt, fruit cups, juices, those sorts of things. In that case, no I don't offer them a snack."

Parent: "Oh, I didn't know all of that. Is that true? She asked her son, who agreed. See, you didn't tell me all of that.

That's a different story."

You know it's a pressuring feeling, I'm sure, when a provider is asked by a child can they have a snack to take home with them. Because, the only thing they're going to get when they go home is a sandwich or a bowl of cereal, or, nothing at all—but a good night.

Maybe they're acting hoggish. Perhaps they're just doing what they were told to do. I've experienced that many times when the parents tell their kids; 'you better eat there, cause I ain't cooking you nothing.

Provider: "Okay, see you tomorrow."

The family: "Bye."

Child: "Mom, dad, can I have some cookies? Mom, dad can we go to McDonalds? Can I have a juicy when I get home?

Before you'd hear that door close, you'd hear the parent telling the child to ask the provider. They'll do it too. Some of the kids are slick about it. They'll wait until their parents come to pick them up and ask for something you've already said they couldn't have.

Then, the parent would get all itchy bitchy about it. They'd either grab the child by the arm, or shove, push, pop 'em upside the head, snapping about what they can get when they get home. Since they had whatever it was that they were asking for. I remember this happening to me once, twice, all the time.

But, this particular scenario the parent said: "Go get in the car. You can get it when you get home. You got that at your own house."

"No we don't!" her kids yelled out.

My kids and I were peeking out one of the windows, cracking up.

Child: "Can I have some more chicken?"
Provider: "I told you no. You already had some."
Child: "Mommy, I want some more."
Child2: "Please can I have some more."
Provider: "I told you no. You ate. It's time for you to go home."
Parent: "Come on. Get ch'all butts in the car. You got food at home. What chew keep askin' for Shit?"

I just don't understand it. It makes things awkward. When a parent shows intimidation, or a sense of insecurity about their child not having their way at daycare. The kids come back the next day, as if they're not allowed to talk or they'll get in trouble. The parent has the cold shoulder. It doesn't always happen.

Recalling a time when a parent wanted to have a meeting with me over how she is raising her son and feel as though I was to follow suit, makes me cringe with attitude. She was raising her son who wasn't yet a teenager, that he's a man and everyone should treat him like that.

"He's a man, Miss Peggy. If he wants gravy on his food, you suppose to make it for him. It's only grease, flour and water."

When it's more than one parent in your facility who behaves in that manner, it stands out. It's so petty and ridiculous.

It's sad. I love to meet and listen to other providers, telling stories of things that they're going through. It's like a breathtaking moment. I want to shout: **Yes! You're fools too. Just like me**. And still doing daycare.

Some of the parents are like farts. The kind of farts, when you're in a crowded, narrow place, or an elevator, a cramped hallway and someone step on your foot in rotation. You try to suck up the aching throb, then, suddenly someone passes gas. You sharply look in their direction as if you're half pass crazy. No . . . you . . . didn't!

"If I don't . . . get . . . out . . . . of here, right now—we gone have a problem." That's the reaction you'd have dealing with some of these parents. The farts. Some of them. You have categorize them.

There's some providers that'll speak their mind, especially the more age mature. "Don't come over here with no bull. I'll let your ass go." I said that's what some say, Ms. Bernie. And many more that I have met. I wish I could be straight forward like that. Perhaps speaking different choices of words in person. Well, during business hours I try to watch my mouth, reactions and all. After business hours—umm.

Unless they were as brazen as some of the comments I heard from some parents, whom had a lot to say about the meal issues at daycares, particularly home daycares. Then, I'd be like—**lets get ready to rum . . . ble.**

Seriously, although I've written some who said, we know that there's many whom believes in every word, living by each word.

Somebody: "Now, I ain't gon' lie, when I pick up my kids from daycare, I don't have no intentions on cooking no dinner—especially if it's five or six o'clock."

Provider: "If they're suppose to leave at that time, why would you expect them to eat at someone else's house?"

Somebody: "What! If you're cooking dinner or have dinner ready on time and your daycare kids, my kids are still there, I would assume they've eaten."

Provider: "Why would you assume that your child suppose eat there, instead of at home?"

Another: "I'ma tell you like it is. If I come there and notice that, you have food cooked and sitting on your stove and my kids didn't eat, I'll probably get pissed. Eventually, I'll switch daycares if it's a constant thing. Because, I'd be wondering why didn't you feed my kids. Why do I have to go home to cook? When, you already had cooked. They could have ate at your house."

Provider: "So, you're trying to say, that, your provider is responsible for feeding your child every meal?"

Somebody: "Hell yeah, that's what y'all getting paid for?"

Provider: "Wow. So tell me this, if you pick your child up around four and they told you, that, they just had a fruit and a sandwich, would you still plan on cooking dinner?"

Somebody: "For what? That was late enough and good enough. I could see if I picked up around two or three o'clock in the afternoon. But, eatin' anything after four, I'm not cooking nothing."

Another: "I know that's right. The best they'll get when they get home is another sandwich or some cookies. Something like that."

Somebody: "You know what I mean. People don't know how hard it is going to work, then having to get off of work to come home cook, clean, do homework and go through some bullshit with yo teenagers, bills and yo man. That's too much. Eliminate all of that. I need time to myself."

Another: "I figure it's only human to feed someone, if they're in your house."

I don't mean to be over exaggerated about meal time. It's just what goes on. You have to be prepared for uneventful moments. Something as generous as feeding another person, could change your life, literally.

Before I could focus good enough to finish this book, this slight economy wavering that's going on, is going to be in a full recession. It's only going to get worse. Excuse me if I'm wrong.

You can see it though. If you running any kind of business or you're a home owner—nothing is more visible. A childcare provider, who's paying attention to what's going on in his/her at home business, needs to start revising some rules.

They have a food program, which they offer to reimburse you, for money spent. Although, they tell you how much each meal is worth. They too, don't allow a certain amount of meals. Considering they'll pay 2 meals and a snack, or just two snacks, for any one child.

When you look at it, they're really not refunding anything to you. The program is just another person trying to tell you how to run your self-employed at home business.

Don't get me wrong, it's a fine program for the one open to that negotiation. The concern is this; let me feed them—don't tell me what I supposed to purchase and serve. Now, I can go for, one of these food items must be served with at least one of these meals, you're claiming funding for. I can go for not having the same thing everyday. I definitely agree with the limitations on the amount of times out of the week, sweets, chips, candy etc is served.

Telling people that these foods have to be pretty much freshly cooked, daily—outrageous. I was told at one time that, if a child is in my care during lunch and I serve a meal that's also being prepared for dinner, I won't get paid. It was said that I'd be serving the same meal, which they don't allow children to eat the same meal twice in a row.

We have a full time shift. The families leave these kids in our homes, slash business between 9 to 13 hours a day. Children are in and out of these properties morning, noon and night. At least three meals are served and countless snacks throughout the day.

Do you think someone have the patience, time and or money to accommodate such a request? We're not a restaurant.

We suppose to be teaching, loving, taking and picking up from school, taking to bus stops, doing our schedules, menus, payroll, trying to keep our sanity. I mean, I can keep going. The point is we don't supposed to be just standing over the stove and running to the microwave.

I recall telling one of my workers at the time, the reason for me letting go of one of the infants I was caring for.

"Where's the little baby?" she asked as she requested her file from me.

"I had to let her go."

"Why? She was so pretty and always reaching out to you."

"Her mom never wanted to bring her anything over but two bottles. When I would bring it to her attention, that she had to bring her daughter over more than two bottles, she got defensive. She would say, she was told that I was on the food program—that I was suppose to supply her baby meals."

"She's right. You're on the food supplemental program, you have to serve the meals"

"Not no infant formula."

"Yes. That too. If that's what the baby eats, that's what you supply."

"That formula along would take up the entire little check. And these parents get WIC."

"You were wrong. They could ask for that money back. If they find out you're not supplying all the children on your enrollment their meals. You'll have to reimburse them"

PHASE FOUR

WHO'S IN CHARGE? STOP PLAYING WITH MY MONEY

We got notice that the case workers that came to do our semi-annual and annual inspections of our daycare facility and the up keep of our records, were going to be determining, if necessary, if we stay open or not.

If said case worker found anything wrong, they could reject you getting paid for that day, week or month. I think some of those workers got the memo wrong. The new rules had to be reiterated to them.

Some of these workers were walking in and through providers house like "Bitch Move. Get Out The Way." You not Ludacris. Seriously, there were some acting like they were just promoted to FBI—CIA status—acting like they were got damn SWAT.

Eight forty five, that's what time it was. I was sending the kids off to school, mine. I gave them a hug. I told them all; "I love you." I'm shifty minded, though.

I closed the front door. I walked to the side window, to watch my kids walk to the bus stop—until I couldn't see them. Which meant when they turned the corner off of our street. I saw it again.

It's a powder blue car sitting at the end of the street. I'm leery about where it's parked. This is a small street. All the neighbors vehicles, and visitors are pretty much known.

Where it's parked, no one parks. It's the extension of a neighbor on the opposite street yard. I never seen this vehicle before, until two days ago. Now I see it again. I hope it's not being turned over to the drug dealers.

Hmm, I don't know but, I'm watching my kids. It's still there when I leave 30 minutes later to take my daycare kids to their bus stop and school—just like it was a 2 days previously.

"What! No Way! Is this someone for daycare?" I said aloud. It's two weeks later, from the time someone had requested to meet me, for service. Someone is knocking at my door. I looked out of the front door window. I saw nothing. I looked out of my side window, I saw that dang powder blue car again—only thing is, it's right in front of my eyes.

"Hi. Good Morning."

"I came for your inspection."

"Oh, ok. You're my new worker?" She was really evil faced. She said yes and with an attitude and already pushing open my door, she asked if she could come in. I looked at her strangely as she brushed passed me, snorting and rolling her eyes—she smelled like liquor.

After she inspected the lower level—the basement, I asked her would she like something to drink.

"Would you like something to drink?"

"Something like what?"

"Umm, juice, soda, milk, water."

"You have bottled water?"

"No."

She began opening and closing doors off of the kitchen and checking the temperature of the hot water in the kitchen and the bathroom off of the kitchen. Then she got to the back cabinet.

"What's in here?"

"Food."

She opened the double paneled wood doors.

"I asked you if you had any bottled waters. You told me no. But, you got all of this juice and pop back here." She in an upset voice.

"Would you like one? I did ask you I believe if you wanted something to drink." I informed her, with a frown on my face.

"And, I told you I didn't want anything to drink. You got all of that sugar back there. That's not good for your kidneys. You need to invest in some bottled water."

I am just amazed. I'm uncomfortable. This stranger is coming in my house looking through my things, complaining. Now, we go upstairs. I stopped in my tracks as she went in the kids room.

"Why does she have all of these clothes?"

"Huh, excuse me?" I asked puzzled. What business is it of hers.

"Look at all of these clothes hanging in here."

She began sliding the hanging clothes, like she was shopping.

"Why are all of these posters hanging on the wall?" She asked while she traveled her short stocky self across to the other side of the room—delegating—questioning me on privileges I seem to give to my own kids in her eyes. I'm going to poke them out in a minute I thought.

With a chuckle I asked why.

"You want to check the smoke detectors?"

She walk passed me like she didn't hear me.

"Who room is this?" She jumped. I had pressed the testing button anyway.

"Who room is this she asked again?"

"My son. Why, what's wrong?"

"You bought him a bedroom set? How old is he?"

"My only son. We have to go downstairs. The little ones went down already."

She kept snorting, ignoring and irritating me. Then she pissed me off. No, I mean, I can't spell that many curse words, to express how I was feeling. I wouldn't even know how to make sense of the words that I refrain from saying, when she told me that she wasn't going to allow me to get paid, unless I do as she say and get what she wanted me to have in my house.

When I received my inspection report in the mail—I wanted to quit. There's just things you don't do, when you're welcomed into someone's house. Not even welcomed, I allowed these strangers to walk around and look in areas of none of their concern, or business. It's a protocol we have to go through, that needs to be readjusted.

"Where's the toys you supposed to have for them to play with?"

"Right there. Over there. Right here."

"How are they going to have fun with that kind of stuff?"

"Is there something wrong? Should we be doing this another time? You're asking me things that doesn't have anything to do with your inspection." I said with an exhale of giggles in between questions and statements. I didn't want to come off as if I had an attitude.

"It has everything to do with my visit. I'm the one paying you. And, you not getting paid."

"Wait a minute. My toys suits what I do. There's nothing wrong with my toys. I teach here. Those toys over there are stuff characters that talks and tells the kids their colors, shapes, numbers and Spanish. There's a toy chest with dolls and dress up clothes, cars, wrestling men everything. What. I don't get it."

You all don't understand. This lady really wasn't doing what she suppose to be there doing; which was checking to see if I'm doing my recordkeeping; menus; kids have no excess to anything dangerous; checking the smoke detectives and fire extinguisher.

She suppose to make sure I had the appropriate sleeping arrangements, which was cots, playpens and at the time sleeping bags and or mats.

"Where's your furniture?"

"Here's my folders. You can sit at this table."

"I said where's your furniture? Where do your parents sit when they come over?"

"I do daycare and I have tables, chairs and cots for my daycare kids. I don't have to have any furniture."

"As long as I'm your worker you do. I'll write you up every time and you won't be getting paid." She said now while sitting her simple ass down at the dining room table, going through my contracts, sign in sheets and first aid kit.

She was back up—prancing.

"So, where does your company sit when they come over; your kids, where do you sit? When these families come to your house they have to have somewhere to sit."

"We sit where we want. They . . . my company sits where I tell them to. Any parent that comes over here, like in any daycare center or school, sits in an available chair. All of this is irrelevant. This shouldn't even concern you."

"You can come sign this verification of my findings of my inspection I did today."

"I'm not signing nothing." I said in a calm voice.

"Oh, it just says you in compliance. But, you still not going to get paid, unless you get some furniture in every room. If I come out here and you don't have any furniture, you won't get paid for that whole week. For now, you in compliance. You're missing some things in your 1st aid kit but, I didn't write you up for it. You need to get some more safety pins and batteries in your flashlight, that's all."

I signed it. I smiled, walked her to the side door and said;

"Thank you take care" with a frown on my face. I left a message for her manager or supervisor to call me back. They didn't.

But, two weeks later when I got a copy of my inspection report in the mail, I left another message. I got a call back in a matter of hours.

Unfortunately, I had to go over her head. Then, I had to go over her supervisor's head. Next it was over his head during another situation.

Message: I need for someone to contact me at 640-* * * or I could give you the number to my attorney. I just received a copy of my inspection report and it's all lies on here.

I'm not about to lose my license for some drunk psycho. She came in my house disrespectful. She was asking me personal questions, that had nothing to do with daycare.

She's telling me what to do with my money and how she wants me to spend it. That, if I don't she's going to revoke my license and deny me payment.

I . . . will . . . press charges. She already came in my house smelling of liquor. She was ignoring me. She wouldn't respond to nothing I said. She wouldn't give me her full name.

I signed a paper saying one thing which was that I was incompliance. Yet, I get a copy that says something totally different! Somebody better call me now! Somebody better come to my house and do that damn inspection over. She better not ever come back in my house.

"Good Morning, Miss. Lee."

"Good Morning" I said with an attitude, like he did it.

"Relax. Calm down. I heard the anxiety in your voice on my messages and I hear the tension in it now. Take a deep breath. Tell me what's going on, so that I can help you."

I told him over again how she behaved when she came to do my inspection.

"But, to send me notification that, I was out of compliance. It has on here, I had clothes strewn throughout my house—umm, that, it was puddles of water on the floor. I think it had that, I didn't have adequate toys. It was bull. That's what I know."

"So, you're telling me that this isn't true?"

"What!"

"I'm just asking, Miss. Lee."

"No, it's not. The only thing on my floors, is carpet and the furniture that sits on it. And, my daughter pajama pants that was on the floor, in her bedroom, in front of her bed. But, every room was clean."

"So, it was in her room."

"Yes."

"I'm just asking. It's beside the point. Pajamas on the floor has nothing to do with daycare. What about the water?"

"Where would puddles of water be? No, it wasn't any water on my floors. Here's the thing, my house would never be like that for one. Secondly, I knew I was up for inspection and was told a time frame. Why would I have my house like that? It wouldn't be like that anyway—still."

"You don't need to worry about this. I'm going to talk to her. We'll see how it goes the next time."

"Next time! Oh no. She can't come back in my house. I want a new worker. I'm reporting her."

"Now . . . now wait. How am I going to talk to her and see if she does better. You have to try and understand. Give a person a second chance. She's going through something."

"I'm sorry. That has nothing to do with me, though."

"You don't want to lose your job. I know you don't want her to lose hers. Let's try to be considerate to others Miss. Lee."

"Are you serious? I really want to know, are you being serious? Because, she doesn't have to lose her job—she better lose my address. She can't come back over here. I'll end up hurting her in my house. I think you lost your mind, too."

He started chuckling, clearing his voice.

"I don't want to put people business out here, but, when individuals have been on a job as long as some—we want to show them support. We don't want to drag them further down. This particle employee had to face some difficult challenges. Amongst, that, burying a parent. So, let's see how it goes when she comes back out later this week or next week."

"What!! Why! I said no!"

"Miss. Lee how are we going to know how she's performing if she doesn't come back out? You're out of compliance. She has to come and check to see if everything was corrected."

"It was a fucking lie!"

I ended up having to call his boss or supervisor. I wanted to cry. At least he told me to write down everything, that, it was unacceptable. I agreed I didn't want her to lose her job, but, coming back to my house, will get her ass whooped.

They sent someone from another agency to come and check for the correction of her bogus claims.

"We'll send someone else out there to check."

"It's a lie."

“She probably made a mistake and put someone else’s information on the wrong forms. We’re just going to do a new inspection. Just checking those areas. But, can we agree to have her come out to your home on the next visit so that we can document her performance?”

“Yes.”

I said yes. But, in my mind, they took it under consideration that it was an accurate documentation. It was a lie. So, “F” you, too.

I left a message for the director of the childcare program, later. She can’t come back to my house. I don’t trust her. She’s a liar. She’s negative and troubled. That woman is a stranger and made me uncomfortable. This wasn’t going to be a feeling, that, I was going to have in my own dang gone house.

I did what they requested me too do. This loopy duck comes back to my house months later. Twice she came back on some cockamamie diva bullshit.

Yes, I know stop using foul language. But, to go back in my mind and remember those visits, I feel like I'm there again.

She knocked on my side door. As always, I greeted with a smile and a chirpy demeanor.

"Good Morning." I greeted as I held the screen door open for her.

Again, she brushed passed me. Doesn't seem like she changed.

"Hi." she said as she went up the stairs to the kitchen.

We went over the paperwork, first. Other workers I've had inspected the house first and then sat down to go over the files—whatever.

"What did I tell you to have and I wanted to see, when I came I came back out here?"

"Um, what, the safety pins, for the first aid kit. I showed them to you."

"Where's your furniture? I told you I wasn't going to pay you, until you get some. Other people need to have somewhere to sit."

"You can't stop me from getting paid. I don't have to have any furniture, for my company. Why you worried about it? Here's toddler tables and chairs for little ones. Here's tables and chairs for older ones. I have mats. These are the same things that they have in the schools."

"But, you not a school. Where does you and your kids sit?" she asked as we walked down the stairs to do the inspection for the basement—checking the smoke detectors and making sure nothing is around the furnace and hot water heater.

"Where are you going?" I asked as I went up the steps leading to the main level of the house and heard the side door squeaking open.

"When you do what I say, then, I'll give you your inspection. You know if you don't get an inspection done your license will be revoked."

"You have to finish my inspection. You can't just leave. I'm telling."

Then, I got a letter in the mail from her. Again, threatening me that she was going to have my license revoked and stopping payment. The letter said something about my phone being disconnected. It's a requirement that all type b childcare providers have a working phone in their house at all times. I'm assuming centers also.

Message; Hi. This is Peggy Lee. I'm a type b childcare provider. I was calling because I received a letter in the mail, stating that I was going to lose my license. Because, I don't have a working telephone line in my house. The number that you have on this letter, I haven't had for like, two years. My current number is the same as the one you've used so far on several occasions and that's 640-* * *. Please call me back as soon as possible. Thanks a bunch.

I never got a phone call. Instead, one day I saw some figures out in front of my house. I heard the knock on the side entrance.

It was her with a jolly green giant.

"Hi."

"Hi. I'm coming to check your phone line, to see if it's operating."

"Oh, okay. Who is that, behind you?"

"This is my co-worker. She introduced her."

"Is there anyone else out here? And, what's the purpose of her coming into my house?"

"No, it's just us. I just have her as my witness to verify that I'm checking your phone line."

My linguine brained worker was acting half way decent, although she was out of line.

They came up. I showed her the phone and picked up the receiver so that she could her the dial tone.

"No." she said as she took the receiver out of my hand—hanging it up without even listening.

She flipped her hands and snapped her fingers to her flunky—dumb dizzy dumb, who pulled out her cell phone.

"What's the number?"

"What number?"

"Your phone number."

I said my number. She told me to say it slow. That was for her co-worker's sake.

"Why am I giving my number to her? I don't know her."

She didn't respond. She stood there. I gave her the number.

"You want me to answer it too?" I laughed out loud. She starred at me like I was crazy. The phone began to ring. I laughed and right in front of them, I picked up the receiver.

"Hello."

She walked passed me peeked in the other room and walked out of my house, without saying a word.

Yes, I reported that. I was told I should had told her to get her ass out of my house.

“That’s why you providers need to familiarize yourselves with the rule book. You point out or have whomever comes out to your house to point out whatever procedure and rules that needs to be followed and understood. Anything else, you tell them to get out.

You still have to maintain control. That’s your business, your show.”

I heard him. He was correct. But, I also know when it comes down to it, those county workers are going to be heard, not us.

Even if we were in our rights to tell one of them to leave, like I wanted to at another time with a different county worker.

I’d face a hearing.

Someone was coming over to drop off some groceries or pick some up. My new worker was sitting at the table. I introduced the two. She was fanning her hand all about, like something was flying around her. Now, I know she was dismissing the introduction.

"Oh, hi. But, you got to go. You can't stay here."

I was beyond displaced with myself in my own house.

Our faces spoke a thousands words.

"Oh, you can stay. What's your name? Let see if you're the list of visitors allowed to be on the property.

Afterwards, I nicely confronted her.

"Do you think that was appropriate for you to do? You could had addressed me when they left. You don't have no right to kick no one out of my house."

"I'm just letting you know. Y'all can't have nobody that's not on your list of people who can be in your house, while you have daycare kids here. They have to be finger printed and approved."

"That still wasn't your place."

"Look, it's about to be a whole lot of changes. The agency is enforcing these rules. I'm not going to be here long. I want you all to get it right. Don't say I didn't inform you. They taking these licenses."

She was out of line in that situation, but she was a nice, jazzy, informative, personal worker. She came after that damn troll head.

If it's not the parents coming in wanting a discount, for no apparent reason, already cutting into your income before they even start good—it's your county worker.

I'd have a parent come in and do the meet and greet. The next thing you know questioning of if they can get a prorate when they start, since they're coming in the middle of the week.

No, I'd have to tell them. If I prorate it then, I'd have to do the same thing later. Sometimes they don't come back. That's okay, too.

These parents can't pay me enough. They don't pay me enough.

My rule is this; all payments are due for the entire week, on the first day of the work week—Monday. If you don't show. You don't show. I work from home. I'm always here. I don't do refunds.

When you have available slots, and each one is filled because someone is paying you, no one else can fill them. If you wish to prorate it, you'll never have a business.

You'll never be able to pay your bills or up keep your household.

Because rest assure, they'd continue to half ass show up so they don't have to pay full price.

I lost a lot of business like that. But, hey the business is not worth obtaining if that's what you have to look forward to.

Like, when some of these workers come out to your house, you don't look forward to them coming out. It seems as if they're trying to keep you out of compliance, instead of making sure you are in compliance. Of course, money is mentioned.

"Oh . . . well, everything's looks ok. Wait, what is this?"

"What is what?"

"Is that a hole in the wall?"

"Where?" I asked. I noticed her looking behind a bedroom door.

I didn't know it was there. But, it was. I didn't have a door stopper. So, there was a door knob print in the wall.

"Oh my goodness! I didn't notice. I'll have this fixed in 2 minutes. I'll be right back. I have to go in the basement to get the mesh tape and spackle. I have paper on the table."

"I'm going to have to write you up for that. You can't fix that while I'm here. You know that hole can jeopardize your license?"

"I didn't know it was there. I'm about to fix it?

"You can't. I'm already here. I'mma just have to write you up."

That was crazy, considering she just got there. We didn't do any paperwork yet. We didn't do the other floor, for inspection. I was pissed the 'F' off.

The purpose for them coming to your house is to make sure everything is in order. Not to keep you down, but to make sure you stay up and together. Doesn't it all effect their status, if we're (provider) not in order, in compliance?

Yes, yes, yes. Report, report, I did.

"My worker came out to my house. I didn't know it was a hole in the wall. It was a hole in the wall behind a door, from someone perhaps barging through, or pushing up hard against it. I don't know. I wanted to fix it. She said I couldn't.

She was more so interested in writing me up and coming back out, than making sure I have everything in order, right then and there. Don't send no one out to my house that's trying to drown me.

We supposed to be excited, at least content with these people coming out to our house. We're running a business, so we need them to let us know if all is in order."

"You're right. Let me see what's going on."

I received a call from her.

"Miss. Lee, I was told to call you. You called my supervisor?"

"Yes, I did." I said it all nonchalant.

"For what?"

"I called him about the hole in the wall, that, I fixed."

"Ok. So, you fixed it. I told you I would be coming back out when you fixed it. Or by the deadline that was sent out to you."

"Well, it was fixed five minutes after you left. So, I called to let him know."

"What else did you say to him?"

"I don't know. I was talking to him?"

She came out a couple of days later—looked at the wall and left—in one minute exact.

It's important that these people come out to our facilities. They're strangers still, who shouldn't have to go through your entire house, looking through everyone's closets, bathroom closets, that's not apart of daycare. It's intruding.

I recall one of my workers that I had, ask me why did I have so many bottles of perfume. Having these strangers coming into your home slash business, could cause problems. They could be judging you off of materialistic things, going back telling what's in your house, where things are located.

They say that we're self-employed childcare workers. Yet, these county workers that comes out to your house, and other county officials have more say so over your business, that's in your house, then yourself.

It's a rule in place right now, that states you have to have at least six consecutive hours to yourself. That's fine. One has to have a sanity break, but, let it be under our own discretion. Allow us to be able to fill a slot, during the needed times, without having to ask to switch schedules.

Right now we can work pretty much eighteen hours a day, but a set shift or shifts, that's leaving six hours left for ourselves. That's interfering with availability and possible income.

I wanted and needed to add children/families to my shifts. A family needed hours from 10am thru 8am. I couldn't accept them, since the hours went into my six hours to myself.

That's when the case workers should get involved. When they look and go through the families that's in your care, noticing the hours and days. Not seeing the provider with at least six to eight hours out of that week to themselves, that's when the case worker should interfere and say cut back or let go.

We shouldn't have to ask permission to change our schedules or we'll get in trouble.

Who's in charge? Or, who's trying to be in control and manipulate?

We as childcare providers must be the ones in charge. We can't afford for someone else to try to take over what's also our homes. We have to be the ones in charge. We're the ones struggling to up keep a business of families with troubles, struggles and problems. We have our own families. There has to be room for decisions and choices. This is how we make our money.

Loving the children and some families, is great. At the end of the day, providers have to still generate an income. An open schedule is needed. Six hours of personal time out of the week, is a must. I believe in that.

Providers has to be the ones in charge of that schedule, that timeline. Hours consist of money. Money consist of being able to replace equipment, get supplies, pay utility bills that's more higher than a person working outside of home since providers are using more of their utilities than an average working family. It's pricey.

They don't inform us of grants any longer, donations that they may have, to help us out. They didn't even give us a supply of the receipt rolls for the new machines. Just more out of pocket expenses we have to spend.

So, like anyone else we have to work hard and get that extra shift. Hell, my carpet needs replacing. But, I can't take on another shift, without asking to do so. It'll go into those six hours.

I need things for the kids to learn. I teach my kids. I'm sure, I hope that other provider does the same. But, we keep getting these drops in pay and request to teach the kids, do the continuing education hours, that we now must pay for.

Hours have even changed. Requirements for a provider to care for someone's children as of now, is degrading. Many families come to a home childcare provider with 60 hours a week. We don't get paid over time unless it's over 60 plus hours.

The pay amount for an infant . . . an infant is under $140 a week and the baby is in your house/daycare a minimum of 10 hours a day—5 or 6 days out of a week.

If we do five days at that price, which I told you it's less, we get paid like $28 dollars a day, for a 10 hour or more shift. I guess we supposed to add up all the kids we have and balance, budget and figure the amount of pay that'll way.

That's fine. But, it's still not enough. We need room to grow. All these schools are closing and we can't have a drive or a sale of some of the equipment, especially from the preschools. The kids have to have a setting that's going to allow them to learn. They have to start learning from the daycares. We're their only hope right now.

This is a business. Just because it's in your home, doesn't mean you supposed to be relaxed on the responsibility and respect of it.

Don't try to get into this line of work thinking, yeah, I'm about to make this amount of money, just by sitting in my house doing nothing.

When those little people leave your household daycare going to another daycare or center for whatever reason and or school, you want a good, respectable assessment coming from your business.

Those little ones are the validation of your business. Their behavior and knowledge, in the next familiar childcare setting and or school dignifies your position as a childcare guidance instructor.

I love being a childcare provider. It's not an easy position. You have all sorts of individuals coming to your home and now what you've made your business.

They come with all of their troubles, their struggles, parenthood woes, children with handicaps and all. You have the parents that's doing exactly what you need for them to do. You'll have joyful moments with the little ones and their family members.

You'll have to conform your maybe judgmental ways in order for your business to be presentable and respectable.

Things could change over night. Don't get too comfortable. Always take time out for yourself and your family. Time doesn't stand still. It moves fast. So, don't miss out on your own life, for no business.

Many of us set in the house keeping others' children. We didn't take a day or a weekend to go study a trade. We didn't go out and seek employment elsewhere, even if just part-time. Now that the times are getting even harder, and the requirements to be an at home childcare provider much demanding—we have no experience to seek work outside of home.

Grow. Don't stand still. Never make this business 'It'. I don't care how old you are. This business is not just the only thing you have. It's not just all you're about.

Again, like it's required for childcare workers to take the continued education hours, it's good, but not fair.

You're only getting approval for certain classes, that they feel you're to take. That too is great. I believe that a person should get accounted hours for their continuing education hours, if they're already enrolled in school, course and or a workshop that can be used to teach the children.

It doesn't work like that. This is why it's important that all providers continue to build their brand—you. We're required to take hours of classes that's appeasing to the county/state. Thus, we're not paid more for acquiring the extra knowledge.

Therefore, if you must take these classes for the agency in order to keep your license or certificate, then, take up something that you always wanted training in so that you could appease your future—during and after you stop doing childcare.

Before you get into this business, know your worth. If you don't know who you are, what you really want out of life, this line of work can interrupt your life and future.

Think about your goals, needs and wants for your family and yourself. When you design the layout of your path of destination and you conclude that a childcare provider is what you're choosing to do—do it well.

Invest in your business. You don't have to have a building, a school or land. You take a room of your house and bring it to daycare life. That atmosphere counts. Set the plans and rules, then take off.

Your presentation of yourself and care you give to these families will be your advertisement.

Always remember not to count on the money or anyone else.

Now that they have these swipe cards out, some of these people act like they have a credit card. You can't swipe it at Macy's. People act like they can. Either it's lost or forgotten.

The longer they don't swipe the more they put you behind in pay and claiming manually.

RULES THAT HAD TO BE REPEATED

These are just some of the rules I had to post. I always made sure it was on the door. There was one door that my families came to. No other door could they go to. That's just a simple way of keeping your business separate from family and home life.

I would post these rules. Yet, every other month or so I would change the color construction paper background, that the white sheet of rules were displayed on.

That was a way of getting their attention. I would inform them to make sure that they read them. It was a way for me to bring to their attention that someone is breaking my rules, without pointing my fingers. I didn't want to make no one person uncomfortable. I wanted to avoid negative, insinuated conversation.

1) All children in pampers are to have enough pampers for the day.
A minimum of 10 in a bag along with wipes for each child in pampers.
2) Any child in pampers must come with a fresh pamper on before dropping off.
3) All children must have a complete clean change of clothes.
4) All children must be picked up on time.
5) If an alternative is picking up a child in the evening hours they must come 2 hours before your scheduled hour of pick up.
6) All private pay is due on Mondays for the entire week. I don't prorate if you choose not to come. I will automatically care for, love and teach your child. You are paying for your slot.
7) County co-pays are due before or on the 1st day of the month. If the 1st ends on a holiday or weekend your pay will be due the weekday before.
8) There's a $15 late fee for late pick ups, every 30 minutes—be it a full 30 minutes or not. So, please pick up on time.
9) Please call if you're running late for drop off. You have within an hour of your scheduled hour of drop off to bring your children to care, unless otherwise agreed upon exception.
10) Please knock and speak before entering facility.
11) No child should bring any toy guns, knives or weapons

12) No entering nor any care without your swipe card.
13) Keep children with you at all times. Children should not go pass the daycare door, in neighbors yard or no where on property.
14) Please use assigned daycare door only. Do not enter other doors on the property, even if it's opened.
15) If your child is suspended or sent home for bad behavior, you can not have them dropped off at daycare. A suspension letter must accompany you in order for any child to be in daycare, during hours and days that they're not schedule to be here.
16) If you have more than one child here, you can not pick up one at a time. If one child is being picked up to go to an appointment and will not be returning, all children must leave at that time. Nevertheless, if any personal appointments are scheduled close to your pick up time, all children must accompany their parent for departure. Ex; your pick up time is at 4pm and your appointment is at 2pm
17) Sorry but you can not use daycare as a visitation point for other parents nor your family social worker
18) No loitering on property

I hope I shed a little light on what you could sometimes expect in this business. If you're already working with children or are preparing to work with children and their families, especially in a home setting, get ready.

You could never be prepared. Always expect the unexpected. Be willing to change and let go.

Know your limitations. If you don't this business, this position will break you, in more ways than one.

Don't forget to keep those journals and incident reports. It could be of an injury, a disagreement or perhaps some weird s* * * you noticed. I don't care how close you become to the families. When those workers come out to your house, make sure they go over that report, also their inspection findings with you before they leave.

Some of them will tell you there's no problem. You're in compliance. You passed the inspection. They'll tell you to sign their little computer—that you agree. When you get a copy in the mail, it'll say you were out of compliance. You're missing something in the 1st aid kit. They didn't see something posted, whatever it may be.

Pay attention and remember; You're in charge.

JOURNAL

INCIDENT REPORT

JOURNAL

INCIDENT REPORT

If this is not what you want to do. If it's something that you can't handle at this time. Let it go. Tell the parents or someone to come and pick up the kids. Many bad things are happening to these kids in the centers, school, home daycares and nanny hired positions.

It's a simple; I can't do this job right now. My mind is not present.

Don't jeopardize no one else's child's life. Not even yours.

I love my position. I can't stand some of the moments. I love it more than I hate it. I hope that you all find enjoyment, along with healthy resolutions to some concerns, in your current or new position as a childcare provider. If not . . . .

It's okay to walk away.

ABOUT THE AUTHOR

Peggy Lee has been doing childcare from her home, for over fifteen years. She wanted to share some personal and heard of stories, to the new comers in the childcare field and to the curious. Peggy Lee still resides in Cleveland Ohio, with her three children.